NEW FEMINIST SCHOLARSHIP

A Guide to Bibliographies

By Jane Williamson

THE FEMINIST PRESS

THE CLEARINGHOUSE ON WOMEN'S STUDIES
OLD WESTBURY, NEW YORK

Library of Congress Cataloging in Publication Data:

Williamson, Jane, 1950–
    New feminist scholarship.
    Includes index.
    1. Women's studies—United States—Bibliography.
2. Feminism—United States—Bibliography.   3. Reference
books—Women.   4. Women's studies—Canada—Bibliography.
5. Feminism—Canada—Bibliography.   I. Title.
Z7161.A1W54   [HQ1180]   016.30141′2′0973   79–11889
ISBN 0-912670-54-1

This book was typeset in Garamond by Talbot Typographics
and printed by Braun-Brumfield on Warren's 50# text stock.

Design by Susan Trowbridge

With special acknowledgment to the Exxon Corporation for
a grant that helped support the publication of this book.

Table of Contents

Acknowledgments

These acknowledgments must begin with Susan Thomson, my teacher at Columbia University, who sponsored the original independent study with which this bibliography began. I would also like to acknowledge the support of Florence Howe and Catharine Stimpson during one phase of this project. I am indebted to Merle Froschl, a wonderful editor and an even better friend; I think she knows how much I appreciate her and her help. A thank you is due to David Porter for his help with the tedious job of proofreading. Finally, my greatest debt is to all my sister bibliographers whose work I have collected and read and enjoyed. Long may they continue.   *J. W.*

How to Use This Book

There should be little problem in finding the desired entries. Author and title indexes have been provided for users looking up a known source; others will be guided by subject arrangement and cross-references. The following points should clear up any confusions.

● Citations follow standard form in most cases. For brevity, if a work has a corporate author/publisher, the organization name is listed only once—as author—and the publisher statement is omitted. Thus, in these cases, the date follows directly after the place. For example:

Business and Professional Women's Foundation. *Sex Role Concepts.* Washington, 1973.

● Place statements have also been kept brief; only the city is listed (not the state), since publishers' full addresses are given at the end of the book.

● Earlier editions of a bibliography or works on which the compilation is based are given at the end of the annotation in parentheses.

● Prices were not included because they change too frequently, so readers are advised to check the price before ordering. A stamped, self-addressed envelope will speed the reply.

● For ERIC publications, order numbers are included in parentheses at the end of each entry, and should be used for prompt service.

● The order addresses for publishers are listed in a separate section at the end of this publication. If there is no publisher included in the citation, the address will be listed under the name of the author.

7

Introduction

New Feminist Scholarship began in 1974 as an independent study project while I was a library school student. Although none of the standard works and sources I was learning about were able to provide much information about women, I knew from my experience in the women's movement and from women's studies courses that there were such materials available. Yet I found not even a suggestion that a large "underground" of bibliography in women's studies existed. I felt it was important to compile all these valuable but obscure sources in order to give support to the growing array of research and researchers in women's studies, as well as to alert the established library world to the existence of this work.

THE GROWTH OF WOMEN'S STUDIES

During the past five years, women's studies has developed tremendously in size and sophistication. Many statistics can be cited to gauge growth in size. Women's studies programs have increased from 112 in 1974 to 301 in 1979.[1] While there were two academic journals devoted to women in 1974, now there are at least five major quarterlies.[2] Research and publications are impossible to count, but the size of this biblio-bibliography provides at least a representative measure—the more bibliographies there are, the more publications there must be. In 1974, *New Feminist Scholarship* included 73 bibliographies, it now includes 391. If one assumes that each bibliography represents an average number of one hundred books, the extent of the growth begins to emerge.

Sophistication is more difficult to document, but here, too, we have some signposts with which to measure the gains. We have seen increased autonomy and legitimacy of women's studies programs, partly through the granting of degrees. There are now 106 institutions where one may pursue a degree in women's studies (80 offer the B.A.; 21 the M.A.; and 5 the Ph.D. or equivalent).[3] The formation of formal associations is another measure of maturity. In addition to many local and state affiliations, there are now two national organizations of prime importance: the National Women's Studies

Association founded in 1977 and the Women's Information Services Network founded in1975.[4] Finally, for what it's worth, women's educational concerns also have received the stamp of approval from the federal government. The Women's Educational Equity Act appropriated $30 million over three years for grants to projects and activities nationwide, a large portion of which was earmarked for the establishment of a national communications network.[5]

As women's studies in all its facets has grown and matured, it has received more attention and acceptance from the "establishment": colleges and universities, publishers, scholars, reviewers. But this is where the real work remains to be done. Integration into the mainstream is not easy on any front, because it is at this point that the dominant group must change. Curriculums, reviewing principles, research priorities, editorial direction must all be overhauled to incorporate feminist ideas.

Bibliographies in women's studies parallel the general trends in the field. There are more bibliographies now than there were in 1974 and, on the whole, they are better. But the majority of bibliographies compiled here still come from informal and noncommercial sources. Less than 50 of the 391 total are the products of commercial publishers. Albert Krichmar's *The Women's Rights Movement in the U.S.* (#346)* was one of the first commercially produced bibliographies; it was published by Scarecrow Press in 1972. Recently, both G.K. Hall and Garland have begun to produce a number of fine bibliographies on women. But changing the library and publishing establishment is a slow process. The current sources of resource tools—individual researchers, women's studies programs, women's organizations and associations, and noncommercial presses—will continue to be the major sources for some time.

SURVEY: BIBLIOGRAPHIES OF BIBLIOGRAPHIES

The first attempt to list available bibliographies on women was made by KNOW press in June of 1971. The *List of Bibliographies on Women and Feminism* (#005) was a free, four-page annotated listing

---

*The number in parentheses following the title refers to the publication's entry in this bibliography; the complete citation will be found there.

of forty-three bibliographies in the following areas: General, Legal and Economic Problems, Employment, Education, Miscellaneous, and Feminist Movement. Ten of the bibliographies from that list have survived and are included in this publication. Most of the remaining entries were mimeographed, stapled sheets available from their compilers—teachers, for the most part, who have long since left the address provided, not to mention run out of copies.

The next efforts were made in 1973—a busy year for bibliographers. The Women's History Research Center published its *Bibliographies on Women Indexed by Topic* (#006) in May of that year. It ran to eight pages and had 188 entries arranged into eighteen topical areas. Approximately thirty of the entries from that compilation will be found here in their original or updated form. Though there were more of them, the bibliographies in this listing were similar in scope and size to the ones in the KNOW list.

The second bibliography of bibliographies produced in 1973 came from Canada. Compiled by Margrit Eichler, *An Annotated Selected Bibliography of Bibliographies on Women* (#002) was published by the Association of Universities and Colleges in Ottawa. It was seventeen pages long and listed more than forty bibliographies. In 1976, Eichler produced a second, revised edition of this compilation (#003), published by KNOW. It was expanded to ninety entries and included all major recent bibliographies. She included only those bibliographies which were readily accessible (i.e., not unpublished, mimeographed lists) and of an acceptable size (fifteen pages or more). Where there were two or more bibliographies on one subject, the more comprehensive one was chosen.

The last bibliography of bibliographies that appeared in 1973 was a masters thesis done by Marsha Koelliker at the School of Library Science, Kent State University (#004). Koelliker gathered together 272 citations to "bibliographies on women published since January 1967 and before December 1972, either separately or within other publications." Of the total, only thirty-three were published separately, the other 259 were published as parts of monographs, anthologies, or journal articles, with articles counting for fifty-five percent.

Finally, the Winter 1977 issue of *Signs* included a review essay on the bibliography of women's studies by Pat Ballou (#001). Ballou discusses approximately sixty bibliographies in the essay section and lists an additional sixty-two. This compilation is the most comprehensive of the bibliographies in this survey and the most interesting to use because of the essay format. Indeed, her article makes fascinating reading for bibliographers of women's studies, as well as feminist scholars, students, editors, and publishers. It is highly recommended.

Pat Ballou makes the following observation in her opening paragraphs: "These bibliographic tools have reflected the materials they listed. As the writings themselves have changed from predominantly action-oriented movement literature to more disciplined academic research, the bibliographies have developed correspondingly from the valiant but often hastily executed products of enthusiastic volunteers to more skillfully edited works." Clearly, the same reflection is true of the bibliography of bibliographies. It would be extremely difficult to produce a solid, scholarly guide to bibliographic sources if there were no solid, scholarly bibliographies to list. The one always reflects the other. And so the biblio-bibliography has grown from the mimeographed, stapled give-away of 1973 to the major review essay in a scholarly journal of 1977 to the publication of *New Feminist Scholarship* in 1979.

SCOPE

New Feminist Scholarship includes 391 bibliographies, resource lists, and literature reviews on women that were published separately or that appeared as periodical articles. It does not pretend to be comprehensive. Indeed, bibliographers of women's studies wrote as early as 1973 that "there is no possibility of compiling a *complete* list of bibliographies written about women."[6] On the other hand, this is not a selective list; that is, I did not attempt to choose the best or biggest in each field. Rather, I listed as many bibliographies as I could find, within certain limits.

Only materials published in English are included—though that does not mean only those of U.S. origin. Out of print sources are listed and are so indicated. They are included for two reasons: one is that they are available in many libraries and remain useful; second is that I wanted this compilation to show the scope and quantity of bibliographic work done in women's studies, to provide an historical perspective.

I have not included general, brief reading lists of basic feminist works, usually give-aways, which have been produced in great numbers by public libraries, women's organizations, local NOW chapters, etc. Their scope is too narrow—they list the same books again and again—and their number is legion. Neither have I included the many excellent lists of nonsexist books for children and young adults. For one thing, I consider them to be outside the scope of this more research-oriented compilation; and again, they are too numerous and frequently too ephemeral to make the compiling worth the effort.[7]

Another category excluded from this compilation is the literary bibliography of individual women writers. While this type of compilation would have fit the general scope requirements, including them would have swelled the literature section beyond proportion. The fact is, there are enough such publications that they deserve a source guide of their own. Finally, I have not included bibliographies that appeared as part of monographs or anthologies.

ARRANGEMENT AND ANNOTATIONS

The citations have been arranged by subject into thirty sections. I have made the headings as straightforward as possible, so that overall, there should be little difficulty in finding the needed items. As I worked, I let the material guide me, creating new sections as they were needed, using five entries as the cut-off point. Each section begins with an explanatory headnote defining the subject and its scope.

There were, of course, a number of problems in categorizing by subject. An overall concern was how to classify the many bibliographies published in Canada. Margrit Eichler's fascinating article on the interplay between feminist research in Canada and feminist research in the United States (#069) convinced me to disperse them throughout according to their subjects, making this a bibliography of U.S. and Canadian bibliographies.

Then there were some individual problems. The only volume on prostitution, for example, seemed to fit nowhere. Ultimately, I put it in with the other professions, rather than in the more usual criminal justice section, as an expression of feminist sentiment on the "criminal" nature of the endeavor. The one bibliography on sports did not seem to warrant its own category; however, since it's an important issue for women, I included it in the health section.

Of the total 391 entries, 215 are annotated, or fifty-two percent. My original intention was to annotate every entry. As I worked, I had to modify my plans. This was due partly to time and partly to availability. In order to speed things, I made yet another decision in that seemingly endless chain of arbitrary choices the bibliographer is faced with: I decided to stop annotating periodical articles. This also was necessary because I continually had problems locating the particular titles or issues. I preferred to concentrate my energies in locating the more substantial, separately-published compilations.

METHODOLOGY

I did not use a conventional methodology for this project because I felt it would not do the field proper justice. The subject under inspection is large and diverse; it does not readily lend itself to methodical searching of indexes, reference guides, abstracts, and so forth. Because most of the bibliographies in women's studies are not produced by mainstream publishers, they are not picked up by standard reference sources and not cataloged by libraries. They have something of a "fugitive" quality about them. They have to be searched for—and hard—but not in the traditional ways.

Nevertheless, there are several sources I have searched thoroughly: *Women Studies Abstracts, The Bibliographic Index,* and Besterman's *World Bibliography of Bibliographies.* The undeniably best source of bibliographies in women's studies, however, is other bibliographies; therefore, I have relied chiefly on my sister bibliographers. Once started on this project, I could have continued forever just following up on the leads from each new source as I found it. This is what makes a project such as this one so interesting. Instead of spending hours tediously copying citations from indexes (though there is some of that), one's time is spent searching library catalogs and special collections, writing endless letters for review copies and citation checks, making phone calls, tracking down details, and always poring over new bibliographies.

Finally, there was the problem of when to quit. A deadline from the publisher obviously gives one a bottom line, but the compiling has to stop early enough to allow for writing the introduction, preparing the index, typing the manuscript, etc. The matter of the missed or unannotated citation must ultimately be accepted as part of the bibliographer's trauma. As Paula Backscheider noted in her introduction to a bibliography of literary criticism (#192): "We know, however, that for every item we found in *The Bath Weekly Chronicle* or the Wales *Western Mail*, we may have overlooked another in *PMLA*. Such is the bibliographer's nightmare." Nightmare indeed. I accept the spectre of incompleteness and would appreciate hearing of those omissions detected by others as well as of new bibliographies as they appear.   *J.W.*

NOTES

1. "Editorial," *Women's Studies Newsletter* 5(3):2, Summer 1977; "Editorial," *Women's Studies Newsletter* 6(4):2, Fall 1978; and "Women's Studies Programs," *Women's Studies Newsletter* 6(4):23–29, Fall 1978.

2. The journals and their dates of first publication are: *Feminist Studies* (1972), *Frontiers* (1975), *Signs* (1975), *University of Michigan Papers in Women's Studies* (1974), and *Women's Studies* (1972).

3. "Editorial," *Women's Studies Newsletter* 6(4):2, Fall 1978.

4. The addresses are: National Women's Studies Association, c/o Women's Studies Program, University of Maryland, College Park, MD 20742 and Women's Information Services Network, P.O. Box 31625, San Francisco, CA 94131.

5. Women's Educational Equity Communications Network, 1855 Folsom St., San Francisco, CA 94103.

6. Women's History Research Center. *Bibliographies on Women Indexed by Topic*. Berkeley, 1973.

7. A good source for nonsexist reading lists and teaching material is *Feminist Resources for Schools and Colleges* available from The Feminist Press, P.O. Box 334, Old Westbury, NY 11568.

Other Bibliographies
of Bibliographies

This section is not annotated; for a discussion of these bibliographies see the Survey section of the introduction.

001 Ballou, Patricia K. "Review Essay: Bibliographies for Research on Women." *Signs* 3(2):436–450, Winter 1977.

002 Eichler, Margrit. *An Annotated Selected Bibliography of Bibliographies on Women.* Ottawa: Association of Universities and Colleges, 1973. 17pp. Out of print.

003 ———. *An Annotated Selected Bibliography of Bibliographies on Women.* 2d ed. Pittsburgh: KNOW, 1976. 33pp.

004 Koelliker, Marsha. *Bibliographies on Women, 1967-1973.* Kent: Kent State University, School of Library Science, 1973. 62pp.

005 *List of Bibliographies on Women and Feminism.* Pittsburgh: KNOW, 1971. 4pp. Out of print.

006 Women's History Research Center. *Bibliographies on Women Indexed by Topic.* Berkeley, 1973. 8pp. Out of print.

General

With sixty-two entries, the General section is the largest and most diverse one. Bibliographies listed here include sources on a wide range of topics. Some of them are research oriented, others are intended for the activist. They include out-of-print compilations from the early part of the century, major efforts on microfilm, and selected lists of as few as four pages. There are bibliographies of periodicals, periodical articles, and government documents as well as of books. There were enough general bibliographies based on the collections of college or university libraries to warrant a separate listing. Compiled by a librarian, faculty member, or student, this type of bibliography is intended first to be a research aid for the local population. Ultimately, however, it is also of interest to those outside the home campus. It can serve as a model for other bibliographers interested in preparing such aids for their own students; it may also be of use to the researcher as well as to acquisitions and interlibrary loan librarians at other campuses.

007 Angrist, Shirley S. "Review Essay: An Overview." *Signs* 1(1): 175–184, Autumn 1975.

008 Armstrong, Douglas and Marian Dworaczek. *Women: A Bibliography of Materials Held in the Research Library*. Toronto: Ontario Ministry of Labour, Research Library, 1974. 81pp. The nearly nine hundred citations in this bibliography are divided into two categories: books and periodical articles.

009 Bruemmer, Linda. "The Condition of Women in Society Today: A Review." *Journal of the National Association for Women Deans, Administrators and Counselors* 33(1):18–22, Fall 1969 and 33(2): 89–95, Winter 1970. A review of the literature from 1966, on the various patterns of life and options in life-style for women today.

010 *Canadian Newsletter of Research on Women*. Vol. I–; May 1972–. The Newsletter began with four objectives: to establish and/or improve communication among researchers; to list ongoing research on the Canadian woman; to list selected relevant research on the international scene; to provide for exchange of ideas. An examination of some recent issues proves

that it has succeeded admirably; it is an unequaled resource for research in progress, bibliography, and book reviews.

011 Cardinale, Susan. *Special Issues of Serials about Women, 1965-1975.* Monticello: Council of Planning Librarians, 1976. 41 pp. This bibliography provides a much needed reference to the myriad special issues of periodicals that have been published about women. Issues containing a special section of two or more articles are included, as are those devoted to topics "intimately linked with women's roles," such as rape or abortion. However, issues devoted to topics which were considered to be of equal concern to men and women, such as child care or divorce, are not included. There will undoubtedly be some disagreement with the editor's judgment on whether a topic concerns women exclusively or not, but in any case, the coverage is broad with more than three hundred issues included. The citations are arranged alphabetically by journal title, and most of them are annotated.

012 Cisler, Lucinda. *Women: A Bibliography.* 6th ed. New York, 1970. 36pp. This partially-annotated bibliography is one of the first women's bibliographies to appear and has been the personal project of Lucinda Cisler through six editions. It is classified into fourteen subject sections, including: Historical Studies; the Law and Politics; Economics, Work and Child Care; Reproduction and Its Control; Women and Socialism. A periodical list is also included. Notations indicate editions in paperback and those worthy of special attention. Much historical material is listed and much that is new.

013 Daniels, Arlene Kaplan. *A Survey of Research Concerns on Women's Issues.* Washington: Association of American Colleges, Project on the Status and Education of Women, 1975. 43pp. Out of print. A comprehensive review of central areas of research relating to women.

014 Davis, Lenwood G. *The Woman in American Society: A Selected Bibliography.* 2d ed. Monticello: Council of Planning Librarians, 1975. 99pp. The second edition of Davis's bibliography appeared only one year after the first. The introduction has

remained virtually unchanged though the compilation has tripled in size. The sections which carry over, General Reference Works, Biography and Autobiography, Books and Periodicals, each are longer by from about fifteen (General Reference) to sixty (Biography and Autobiography) percent. There are four new sections: Selected Women's Organizations, Women College Presidents, Women's Bureau Publications from 1918 to 1971, and Government Documents. None of these additions is explained in the introduction, in fact, the only change mentioned there is the subdivision of the Biography and Autobiography section by race to make locating books on black women easier. The lack of a subject index will cause some problems in using certain sections. (Original edition: Davis, Lenwood G. *The Woman in American Society: A Selected Bibliography*. Monticello: Council of Planning Librarians, 1974. 33pp.)

015 Ehrlich, Carol. *The Conditions of Feminist Research*. Baltimore: Research Group One, 1976. 20pp. This pamphlet reviews and attempts to define what "feminist" research is and should be. It does not include a comprehensive review of the literature, but discusses twenty articles the author feels are important or representative.

016 ———. "Woman Book Industry." *American Journal of Sociology* 78:1030–1044, January 1973. Carol Ehrlich reviews seventeen books in the women's studies area published in 1971 and 1972.

017 Galloway, Sue. "Women." *Wilson Library Bulletin* 47:150–152. October 1972. A highly selective and annotated list of the publications of the women's movement. The selection represents a good cross-section of the best of the different kinds of publications available. Several sources for comprehensive lists of the periodicals are indicated. The annotations are evaluative.

018 Haber, Barbara. *Women in America: A Guide to Books, 1963–1975*. Boston: G.K. Hall, 1978. Haber's *Guide* is an important new addition to the literature. Taking 1963, the publication date of *The Feminist Mystique* as her starting point, she annotates nearly five hundred volumes of current feminist writing up to

1975. In each of the eighteen subject sections, the first several books are annotated at length, followed by a longer list of briefly annotated selections. Each section also has a short introduction. The compilation can stand alone as a core collection for a women's studies library, and it should prove useful to a wide range of users.

019   Halligan, John T. *Women: A Bibliography of Periodical Articles*. Sacramento, 1973. 17pp. Out of print. Halligan's bibliography is a list of more than three hundred articles on women from approximately seventy periodicals published between January 1 and December 31, 1972. The periodicals indexed cover a wide spectrum, but are primarily general literature. The bibliography is in nine subject sections.

020   Harrison, Cynthia Ellen. *Women's Movement Media: A Source Guide*. New York: R.R. Bowker, 1975. 269pp. This is not just a bibliography, but a guide to sources of information of various sorts. It includes approximately 550 descriptions of organizations arranged by function, type, or main interest of group, and what materials they supply. There are five categories: material producers, material collectors, service organizations, government agencies, special interest groups. There are geographic, title, group name, and subject indexes.

021   Hughes, Marija Matich. *The Sexual Barrier: Legal, Medical, Economic and Social Aspects of Sex Discrimination*. Washington: Hughes Press, 1977. 843pp. Marija Hughes has stopped publishing supplements to her original (1970) bibliography and has given us instead this mammoth one-volume compilation of more than eight thousand citations. It covers the literature in English from 1960 to 1975 in seventeen broad subject sections, from aging to economic status to legal status to sex roles. Even though each of these chapters is sub- and sub-subdivided topically, the sheer size of the compilation makes the lack of a subject index problematic. Nevertheless, *The Sexual Barrier* is certain to become a standard source in many libraries. (Original edition: Hughes, Marija Matich. *The Sexual Barrier: Legal and Economic Aspects of Employment*. San Francisco, 1970. 35pp. Supplements, 1971 and 1972.)

022 Joyce, Lynda. *Annotated Bibliography of Women in Rural America; with a Review of the Literature about Women in Rural America, Bibliography of Women in Rural Areas Worldwide, and Resource Material.* University Park: Pennsylvania State University, Agricultural Experiment Station, Department of Agricultural Economics and Rural Sociology, 1976. 62pp. This volume has several components. It begins with a review essay which discusses the literature in the annotated bibliography and presents the pertinent statistical information on the status of the rural woman. The annotated bibliography is a comprehensive compilation of works published on the American rural woman in the twentieth century; it is a straight alphabetical list by author. The same citations are rearranged (minus annotations) by chronology in another section to show trends over time. Then follows a bibliography on rural women outside the United States; it is not comprehensive. The "Bibliographic Addendum" lists works which Joyce was unable to locate and therefore could not annotate, as well as those which are on related issues such as farm life in general or nonrural women. There are two final sections: one of bibliographies, the other of relevant periodicals, historical and current. For the purposes of this project, rural was defined as all open country and places with populations of less than 2,500. Thus, it includes both farm and small town residents. Joyce's bibliography provides invaluable reference for those researching what is essentially a vanishing species: the rural woman.

023 King, Judith D. *Women's Studies Sourcebook: A Comprehensive, Classified Bibliography of Books.* Allendale: Grand Valley State Colleges Library, 1976. 68pp. This large format pamphlet includes nearly thirty-one thousand citations. It is divided into fifty-one subject sections. There is an author/title index.

024 Kusnerz, Peggy Ann and Ann Martin Pollack. *Women: A Select Bibliography.* ERIC, 1975. 42pp. (ED 112 230).

025 Lewis, Edwin C. *Developing Woman's Potential.* Ames: Iowa State University Press, 1968. 58pp. Out of print.

026 Marlow, Carleton H. *Bibliography of American Women, Part I.* Woodbridge: Research Publications, 1975. Because this bibliog-

raphy is on microfilm, I have not examined it. However, descriptions from the producer indicate that it covers the period up to 1904 and lists forty thousand titles. Part II is forthcoming.

027 Mazur, Carol and Sheila Pepper. *Women in Canada 1965 to 1975: A Bibliography*. 2d ed. Hamilton: McMaster University Library Press, 1976. 174pp. The second edition of this bibliography is approximately three times the size of the first and covers an additional three years. It is devoted exclusively to materials on Canadian women, such that general works which might relate to Canadian women as much as any others are not included, nor are international studies which include Canadian women among others. The 1,973 citations are arranged under nearly three hundred subject headings, resulting in something closer to an index than to a chapter arrangement. This is probably the major bibliographic source on the Canadian woman, certainly for the period covered. (Original edition: Harrison, Cynthia. *Women in Canada, 1965–1972: A Bibliography*. Hamilton: McMaster University Library Press, 1973. 51pp.)

028 Moore, Susanne. *First Sampler: A Bibliography of Works on Women at the George Peabody Department of the Enoch Pratt Free Library*. Baltimore: Enoch Pratt Free Library, 1974. 119pp. Out of print. The Peabody Department existed as a separate library from 1858 until it merged with Enoch Pratt in 1966. Moore's bibliography is an attempt to list all of the collection's works on women, most of them from the nineteenth and early twentieth centuries. The approximately six hundred entries are arranged into ten subject sections: art, economics, education, history, law and political science, literature, medicine, philosophy and religion, psychology, sociology and anthropology.

029 New York Public Library. *List of Works in the New York Public Library Relating to Woman*. New York, 1905. 57pp. Out of print.

030 O'Connor, Patricia, Linda Headrick, and Peter Coveney. *Women: A Selected Bibliography*. Springfield: Wittenberg University, 1973. 111pp. The principles of selection for this compilation were to include a sampling of classic works, some

period pieces, and current research, with entries arbitrarily limited to three per author. Arranged into chapters by subject, the citations include Library of Congress classification notations and locations in Ohio libraries. Also included are lists of special issues of periodicals, bibliographies, and special collections. There is an author index.

031   Rothstein, Pauline Marcus. "Women: A Selected Bibliography of Books." *Bulletin of Bibliography* 32:45–54, April/June 1975.

032   Samalonis, Bernice and Earl R. Shaffer. *Some Sources of Bibliographies Pertaining to Women's Studies*. ERIC, 1975. 22pp. (ED 106 707). A listing of periodicals, documents, and books relating to women's studies and feminism in general. *Some Sources* was compiled from a computer printout of ERIC materials covering the past four years. It is not annotated.

033   San Diego State University, Women's Studies Faculty. *Women's Studies Bibliography: Seventy Essential Readings*. San Diego, 1975. 4pp. Out of print. This tiny but attractive pamphlet lists seventy titles which the women's studies faculty felt were "essential for an overview of the scope and promise of women's studies and it [the bibliography] endeavors to delineate the way in which a feminist perspective transforms the approach to traditional disciplines."

034   Schuman, Pat and Gay Detlefson. "Sisterhood Is Serious, An Annotated Bibliography." *Library Journal* 96:2587–2594, September 1, 1971. This bibliography, which is an attempt to select from the mass of material currently available, was compiled for women—librarians and readers—to offer "a brief picture of the spectrum of thought, history, experience and action in the women's movement." The selective list is meant as only a beginning, a jumping-off point. The introduction discusses some of the major issues of the women's movement, gives statistics, and stresses the responsibility of librarians to provide materials for women.

035   *Signs, Journal of Women in Culture and Society*. Vol. I–; Autumn 1975–. *Signs* regularly carries major review essays of the

new scholarship on women. Nearly fifty such bibliographic articles have appeared as of the Summer 1978 issue. This is a fine source which will be of continuing importance. Citations to *Signs* essays will be found throughout in the appropriate subject categories.

036 *Status of Women Bibliography, A Selective Bibliography of Government Publications.* Bowling Green: Bowling Green State University Library, Government Documents Service, 1973. 14pp. Out of print. This is a bibliography of selected government documents which report in some way on the status of women and which were published between 1967 and 1973. There are three sections: Present Status, Changing Status, and Special Concerns. The citations are very brief, giving only title, date, and number of pages.

037 Tobias, Sheila. "The Study of Women." *Choice* 8(10):1295–1304, December 1971.

038 U.S. Library of Congress. *Brief List of References on Woman's Part in the World Today.* Washington, 1921. Out of print.

039 ———. *List of References on Citizenship and Nationality of Women.* Washington, 1931. Out of print.

040 ———. *Select List of References on the Woman of Today.* Washington, 1908. Out of print.

041 Wheeler, Helen. *Womanhood Media Supplement: Additional Current Resources about Women.* Metuchen: Scarecrow Press, 1975. 482pp. The *Supplement* to Helen Wheeler's original 1972 compilation reprints the bulk of the material in that volume and, therefore, supersedes it. The Basic Book Collection lists fiction by author and nonfiction by subject; Non-Book Resources are listed by type of resource. It is a fairly comprehensive listing of current publications. (Original edition: Wheeler, Helen R. *Womanhood Media: Current Resources about Women.* Metuchen: Scarecrow Press, 1972. 335pp.)

042 *Women: A Bibliography of Special Periodical Issues (1960–1975).* Margrit Eichler, John Marecki, and Jennifer Newton, eds.

Toronto: Canadian Newsletter of Research on Women, 1976. 75pp. *See #043 for annotation.*

043 ———. Volume II. Jennifer L. Newton and Carol Zavitz, eds. Toronto: Canadian Newsletter of Research on Women, 1978. 280pp. The first volume of this bibliography lists more than one hundred special issues of periodicals on women, the second nearly five hundred. Both volumes arrange the entries by broad subject area—sixteen in Volume I, eighteen in Volume II—and provide, in addition to title and date, the complete table of contents of each issue. Volume II also includes additional subject guides to special issues on men, rural women, women immigrants, Jewish women, cross-cultural studies, union women, marriage and family. Another special section in Volume II lists seventeen special issues published before 1960.

044 *Women and Society: A Critical Review of the Literature with a Selected Annotated Bibliography.* Len V. Bergstrom and Marie B. Rosenberg, eds. Beverly Hills: Sage Publications, 1975. 360pp. *See #045 for annotation.*

045 ———. Jo Ann Een and Marie B. Rosenberg-Dishman, eds. Beverly Hills: Sage Publications, 1978. 288pp. The first volume of *Women and Society* includes 3,600 entries primarily in the social sciences and humanities. Criteria for selection were that the work be generally authoritative and available and that it constitute "scholarly and applied research efforts." The 1978 edition is an update of the compilation by Rosenberg and Bergstrom which follows the same format, style, purpose and scope. It continues where the first volume left off, beginning with citation number 3,601 and going through number 6,000.

046 *Women Studies Abstracts.* Vol. I—; Winter 1972—. This quarterly journal includes a book review essay, book reviews, and abstracts which are arranged by subject. Additional articles are listed without abstracts.

047 *Women's Work and Women's Studies, 1971.* Kirsten Drake, Dorothy Marks, and Mary Wexford, eds. New York: Barnard College, Women's Center, 1972. 138pp. (Order from KNOW). *See #049 for annotation.*

048 ———, *1972.* Dicki Lou Ellis et al, eds. New York: Barnard College, Women's Center, 1973. 226pp. (Order from KNOW). *See* #049 for annotation.

049 ———, *1973-74.* Barbara Friedman et al, eds. New York: Barnard College, Women's Center, 1975. 370pp. (Order from The Feminist Press). This annual, interdisciplinary bibliography covers the year's scholarship in women's studies, including research in progress. It is partially annotated and classified by subject. The 1973-74 volume will be the last one published.

050 Young, Louise M. "The American Woman at Mid-Century: Bibliographic Essay." *American Review* 11:121-138, December 1961.

051 Zangrando, Joanna Schneider. "Women's Studies in the United States: Approaching Reality." *American Studies International* 14(1):15-36, August 1975. This interdisciplinary literature review and essay, though now somewhat out of date, provides an excellent introduction and comprehensive overview, touching on women's studies "courses, programs, research, resources and resource repositories, publications, and communications networks."

COLLEGE AND UNIVERSITY LIBRARY GUIDES

052 Amato, Katherine J. *Womenstudy: Guides for Research.* Lake Forest: Lake Forest College, Donnelly Library, 1978. 60pp. *Womenstudy* is a compilation of brief research guides on a variety of topics originally prepared individually. Each one follows the same format which includes "Topic Scope," a brief paragraph outlining the major points and themes of the subject; a selected listing of books including the appropriate classification numbers and subject headings to check; listings of articles, bibliographies, indexes, and abstracts. There are author, title, and subject indexes. A nice format for undergraduate and beginning researchers.

053 College of St. Catherine Library. *Women: A Bibliography.* St. Paul, 1967. Out of print.

054   Freeman, Leah. *The Changing Role of Women: A Selected Bibliography.* 3d ed. Sacramento: California State University Library, 1977. 190pp. Freeman compiled the first edition of this bibliography in 1971. It was revised very shortly after, and the second edition appeared in 1972. The third edition is substantially different; for example, it is more than three times as long. It does not represent the complete collection of the Sacramento library, but is rather a selected list through which Freeman has tried to "provide a bibliographic tool enabling students to trace the history and ideas of the women's movement, to bring into focus a vast collage of facts." The citations are organized into twelve subject categories, such as education, employment, women's movement, and history, and one section of reference materials. The final twelve pages list selected subject headings in the California State University Library card catalog.

055   Hoffman, Ruth H. *Women's Bibliography.* Bowling Green: Bowling Green State University, Library, 1972. 64pp. Out of print.

056   Krichmar, Albert. *Women's Studies: A Guide to Publications and Services Available in the Library of the University of California at Santa Barbara and in the Santa Barbara Area.* Santa Barbara: University of California, Library, 1975. 74pp. Out of print. Krichmar's bibliography of the University of California, Santa Barbara collection is a thorough one. In addition to the usual section on reference sources and the subject classified listing of monographs, there are listings of government documents, periodicals, pertinent subject headings, local women's organizations, and women's studies courses. Krichmar also has included an especially detailed chapter on minority women to help the researcher in a difficult area. There are approximately four hundred citations in this pamphlet.

057   Lasky, Jane. "Selected Bibliography of Printed Materials on Women and the Women's Movement in Booth Library." [Eastern Illinois University] *Illinois Libraries* 58(2):145–152, February 1976.

058   Lo, Henrietta Wai-Hing. *Women's Studies: A Bibliography.* Chico: California State University, Library, 1973. Out of print.

059 Massachusetts Institute of Technology, Human Studies Collection. *Women's Studies Bibliography*. Cambridge, 1977.

060 McKim, Joanne. *The Feminist Collection, Neally Library*. Santa Ana: Santa Ana College, Neally Library, 1976. 113pp. Out of print. McKim's bibliography is a fairly substantial one. The monograph section is broken down into more than forty different subject categories from history to aging to literature to women's work. Books listed include those already in the Neally Library (call numbers given) and those uncovered in research and on order. The periodicals list is very brief and provides titles only.

061 McMillan, Pat and Jean Porter. *Woman's World: A Selected Bibliography on Women*. DeKalb: Northern Illinois University Library, 1974. 15pp. This bibliography varies from the others in this section in two ways: first, it includes periodical articles and second, it does not reflect the library's holdings on women overall. Rather, it concentrates in three areas: education, employment, and the status of women. These three areas constitute about eighty percent of the whole; the rest is devoted to reference sources.

062 Pastine, Maureen et al. *Women's Studies Resources*. Omaha: University of Nebraska Library, 1975. 43pp. Out of print. This bibliography can be duplicated from the one available copy in the reference collection at the University of Nebraska, Omaha.

063 Pettingill, Ann H. and Jean D. Barnett. *Women: A Bibliography of Books and Other Materials*. 3d ed. Los Angeles: California State University, J.F.K. Memorial Library, 1976. 41pp. Pettingill and Barnett have organized their bibliography into thirty-nine subject categories with sections on periodicals and sound recordings as well. The more than eight hundred citations represent only a selection of materials from the J.F.K. Library and not a comprehensive listing. There is an author index.

064 Portis, Juanita W. *Women: An Annotated Bibliography Based on the Holdings of California State College, Dominguez Hills*. Dominguez Hills: California State College, Library, 1974. 75pp. This bibliography is arranged by subject into twelve categories

from art to suffrage, the largest of which (thirty pages) is
"History and Condition." The citations are annotated, though
not by the editor; the descriptions come from book reviews or
from the book's introduction. At the end of each subject section
is an annotated listing of microforms.

065   Rothstein, Pauline Marcus. *Women: A Selected Bibliography of
Books.* New York: Herbert Lehman College Library, 1973. 29pp.
Out of print. Unlike most of the bibliographies in this section,
this one is annotated. It lists monographs only and has no
reference/research guide. The major sections are: General, Feminism Today, History, Sociology/Anthropology, Psychology,
Economic and Legal Status, and Biography.

066   Salzer, Elizabeth M. *A Selected Bibliography of Books on
Women in the Libraries of the State University of New York at
Albany.* Albany: State University of New York Libraries, 1972.
222pp. Out of print. This is a simple listing in subject
arrangement of the books about women in the SUNY Albany
library. Omitted are books about women in sports, medical
books on gynecology and obstetrics, literary works by women
unless related to women, and biographies of individual women.
Library of Congress classification notations are given. There is a
corporate author/title index and a personal author/editor index.

067   Sussman, Barbara and Phyllis Kriegel. *Women and the American
Experience; An Annotated Bibliography of Selected Holdings on
Women and Their Work: 1890–1920 Located in the Sarah
Lawrence College Library.* Bronxville: Sarah Lawrence College,
Library, 1975. 20pp. This compilation is in four sections:
bibliographies, monographs, periodicals, and government
documents. It differs from the other bibliographies listed in this
section in that it concentrates on a specific topic as well as within a
time frame. However, it also reflects the collection of the Sarah
Lawrence College Library. The periodicals list is a fairly extensive
one; not every title was for or by women, but a brief annotation
explains the reason for its inclusion.

068   Waibel, Grace T. *Women: A Selected Bibliography and Guide
to Library Resources.* Fresno: California State University Library,
1972. 18pp. Out of print.

Anthropology and Sociology

Anthropology and sociology have been combined because each has too few entries to warrant its own section. The number of entries, however, does not always correspond directly to level of activity. There is a major bibliographic source in anthropology—Jacobs's Women in Perspective. As for sociology, much of the research does not appear in this section, but in the topical area to which the research is tied; sociological methods can be used to study anything and everything—rape, crime, family patterns, etc. This is especially true of the Sex Roles/Sex Differences section.

SEE ALSO: Sex Roles and Sex Differences.

069 Eichler, Margrit. "Review Essay: Sociology of Feminist Research in Canada." *Signs* 3(2):409–422, Winter 1977.

070 Jacobs, Sue-Ellen. *Women in Perspective: A Guide to Cross-Cultural Studies.* Urbana: University of Illinois Press, 1974. 299pp. Before its publication in this edition, *Women in Perspective* was circulated informally in a two-inch thick mimeographed version—an "underground" bibliographic classic, as it has been called. It is in two parts: the first is arranged by geographical area (each one is further divided into texts, general references, and specific places), the second is divided into twenty-seven subject areas. This is a major reference work.

071 Lamphere, Louise. "Review Essay: Anthropology." *Signs* 2(3):612– 627, Spring 1977.

072 Lopata, Helena Znaniecki. "Review Essay: Sociology." *Signs* 2(1):165–176, Autumn 1976.

073 Huber, Joan. "Review Essay: Sociology." *Signs* 1(3):685–698, Spring 1976.

074 Stack, Carol B. et al. "Review Essay: Anthropology." *Signs* 1(1): 147–160, Autumn 1975.

Art and Music

Three of the six bibliographies in this section concern art, women artists, and art history; two encompass women musicians; one deals with women and film. Both of the music bibliographies include biographical information as well.

075 Crowe, Edith L. *Women Artists: A Selected Bibliography of Periodical Material, 1929-1974.* San Jose: San Jose State University, Library, 1974. 22pp. Crowe has searched *Art Index, Women Studies Abstracts,* and *Social Science and Humanities Index* from 1929 (the first year of *Art Index*) to 1974 for articles on women artists. She has arranged the citations into two parts: one for general articles or articles on particular artists, the other for reviews of group exhibitions by women artists. The bibliography includes more than four hundred citations. Available in limited supply to educational institutions only.

076 Hixon, Don L. and Don Hennessee. *Women in Music: A Biobibliography.* Metuchen: Scarecrow Press, 1975. 347pp. *Women in Music* can be used in two ways. First, it is an index to biographical information on women found in nearly fifty major music reference works. Second, because each entry includes place and date of birth and fields of musical activity or specialization, it serves as a quick reference biographical dictionary in itself. Only "classical" musicians have been included. The volume ends with a classified index by field or activity. There are seventy different classifications from accompanists to musicologists to voice teachers.

077 Kowalski, Rosemary Ribich. *Women and Film: A Bibliography.* Metuchen: Scarecrow Press, 1976. 278pp. *Women and Film* contains more than two thousand citations to works in four areas: actors, filmmakers, images of women in film, and film writers/critics. The volume is divided into sections on each of these topics which are in turn subdivided, where appropriate, into historical and reference works, catalogs, and specific works. Many of the citations are to general film materials which contain information on, but are not exclusively about, women. In some cases, the an-

notations point out what pertinent material a general work does have, and/or how to locate it. The usefulness of this approach can be debated either way: on the one hand, it's a bit misleading for the researcher who's already been through the standard sources and is looking for books specifically on women. On the other hand, it's helpful to know which of the more general or standard works would be most useful. Each user must decide for him or herself. There is a fairly extensive subject/name index.

078 Krasilovsky, Alexis Rafael. "Feminism in the Arts: An Interim Bibliography." *Art Forum* 10(10):72–75, June 1972.

079 Orenstein, Gloria Feman. "Review Essay: Art History." *Signs* 1(2):505–526, Winter 1975.

080 Pool, Jeannie G. *Women in Music History: A Research Guide.* New York, 1977. 42pp. Pool's pamphlet begins with "An Essay on the History of Women in Music" and, like the Hixon book (#076), it includes biographical as well as bibliographical information. The bibliography is in eight subject sections: General Books, Books on Individual Women, General Articles, Articles on Individual Women, Approaches to Women in History, Bibliographies, Lists of Women Composers, and Examples of Denial of Women's Creative Abilities. Other resources for women's music are also listed, including periodicals, organizations, and record companies. The biography section includes only those women composers born before 1900. A discography section lists recordings of women's music available as of September 1977. A final section suggests possible research topics.

Child Care

Child care has long been—and will continue to be—an important issue for women. It is good to know that several excellent guides to the research are available.

SEE ALSO: **Marriage and the Family.**

081 Frost, Judith and Miriam Meyers. *Day Care Reference Sources: An Annotated Bibliography*. ERIC, 1970. 35pp. (ED 039 700).

082 Howard, Norma K. *Day Care: An Annotated Bibliography*. Urbana: ERIC Clearinghouse on Early Childhood Education, 1971. 19pp. (ED 052 823). *Supplement 1*, 1972. 59pp. (ED 069 402). *Supplement 2*, 1974. 60pp. (ED 089 884).

083 Hu Teh-wei. *Selected Bibliography on Child Care Evaluation Studies*. Monticello: Council of Planning Librarians, 1973. 9pp. This brief bibliography is arranged into three main divisions: Conceptual Issues, Cost, and Benefits (effectiveness). There is no introduction, so the heading "Conceptual Issues" is not defined. The section contains, however, works on child development, on legislation and government policy, on working mothers. All three sections include substantial numbers of government documents.

084 Lloyd, Diane. *Child Care in the 1970's: A Bibliography*. Monticello: Council of Planning Librarians, 1977. 97pp. This bibliography is the result of a comprehensive review of the literature published since 1970; it is part of an ongoing research project. More than 1,100 citations are arranged by form or subject into fourteen major sections: General; Bibliographies; Guidelines, Handbooks and Manuals; Surveys and Profiles; The Child Care Consumer; Costs, Finances and Economics; Licensure and Standards; Legislation; Child Care Workers; Parent Participation; Program Models and Descriptive Studies; Empirical Research and Evaluation Studies; Measurement, Observation and Evaluation; and Foreign Experience. An extensive and valuable resource.

085 Reif, Nadine. *An Annotated Bibliography of Day Care Reference Materials.* ERIC, 1972. 42pp. (ED 088 609).

086 Wells, Alberta. *Day Care: An Annotated Bibliography.* ERIC, 1971. 367pp. (ED 068 199). *Supplement*, 1971. 121pp. *Supplement*, 1971, 49pp. (ED 068 201).

Collection Guides

This section includes guides to resource collections on women, including major archives, collections of ephemeral material, and special sections of general libraries. The guides range from the three-volume book catalog of a major historical repository to the small bibliography of a pamphlet collection. An important new source for researchers is Hinding's forthcoming national guide to manuscript collections on women.

087 *Catalogue of the Galatea Collection of Books Relating to the History of Woman in the Public Library of the City of Boston.* Boston: Trustees of the Boston Public Library, 1898. 34pp. This is the catalog of Thomas Wentworth Higginson's library on women, which he donated to the Boston Public Library. The nearly one thousand citations are organized according to Higginson's own classification system into nine major subject groupings: Biography, History and Condition of Women, Education, Health and Hygiene, Relations and Comparisons of the Sexes, Rights of Women, Work and Influence of Women, Literature, and Periodicals.

088 Donovan, Lynn Bonfield. "Library Resources: CHS Collections on the History of Women in California." *California Historical Quarterly* 52:81–84, Spring 1973.

089 Hinding, Andrea. *Women's History Sources: A Guide to Archives and Manuscript Collections in the United States.* New York: Bowker, forthcoming.

090 Nilan, Roxanne-Louise. *The Woman Question: An Annotated Guide to the Women's Pamphlet Collection.* Irvine: University of California Library, 1976. 41pp. The Political Pamphlets Collection of the University of California at Irvine has recently been broadened to include pamphlets from the women's movement. This annotated guide cites and describes approximately 150 pamphlets in seventeen subject sections. It will be of use to the collector, both individual and institutional.

091 Nolen, Anita L. "The Feminine Presence: Women's Papers in the Manuscript Division." *Quarterly Journal of the Library of Congress* 32:348-365, October 1975.

092 Radcliffe College. *Arthur and Elizabeth Schlesinger Library on the History of Women in America: The Manuscript Inventories and the Catalogs of Manuscripts, Books, and Pictures.* Boston: G.K. Hall, 1973. Three vols.

093 Scott, Marda and Elizabeth Power. *The Woman's Collection at the University of North Carolina at Greensboro: A Check-List of Holdings.* Greensboro: University of North Carolina, Walter Clinton Jackson Library, 1975. 150pp. The Woman's Collection was started in 1936 when the University at Greensboro was the Woman's College. In 1947, relevant works already held by the library were added to the collection, and in the 1950s nine hundred volumes were added when the valuable private collection of Anthony Ludovici was purchased. The *Check-List* supersedes all previous editions. (Original editions: Hussey, Minnie Middleton. *The Woman's Collection: A Bibliography of Material, 1937-1943.* Greensboro: University of North Carolina, The Woman's College Library, 1944, 121pp. and Hussey, Minnie Middleton. *The Woman's Collection: A Bibliography of Material, 1944-49.* Greensboro: University of North Carolina, Library of the Woman's College, 1950. 110pp).

094 Sophia Smith Collection. *Catalogs of the Sophia Smith Collection, Women's History Archive, Smith College.* Boston: G.K. Hall, 1975. Seven vols.

095 Thoreen, Bonnie. "Women's Reference Collections." *Booklegger* 1(2):18-21. January/February 1974. Thoreen lists and briefly describes twenty-seven collections of primary sources or special subjects relating to women.

096 Wilson, Joan Hoff and Lynn Bonfield Donovan. "Women's History: A Listing of West Coast Archival and Manuscript Sources." *California Historical Quarterly* 55:74-83, September 1976.

Criminal Justice

Awareness of the special needs, situations, and experiences of women has grown to include the woman offender, indicated by the developing body of literature on women in the criminal justice system. The bibliographies listed here all recognize the need for this separate literature and provide access to it. The most comprehensive source is Rosenzweig and Brodsky's The Psychology of the Female Offender.

097 Anderson, Etta A. "The 'Chivalrous' Treatment of the Female Offender in the Arms of the Criminal Justice System: A Review of the Literature." *Social Problems* 23(3):350–357, February 1976.

098 Doleschal, E. "The Female Offender: A Guide to Published Materials." *Crime and Delinquency Literature* 2:639–670, 1970.

099 Goyer-Michaud, Francyne. "The Adult Female Offender: A Selected Bibliography," *Criminal Justice and Behavior* 1(4):340–356, December 1974. This is a comprehensive bibliography of journal articles published in English and French between 1959 and 1974. It lists more than two hundred citations. According to Rosenzweig and Brodsky (#101), this article represents only part of a forthcoming bibliography compiled by Goyer-Michaud and Lise Brunet-Aubrey.

100 Livesey, Sharon. *Survey of Legal Literature on Women Offenders.* Pittsburgh: Entropy Limited, 1975. 16pp. Four broad areas are examined in this survey: women's legal status, the criminal law, what happens to the female offender, and the law on prostitution and rape. The introduction is substantial and describes the literature in some detail. Most of the sixteen pages are devoted to an annotated bibliography of twenty-six citations.

101 Rosenzweig, Marianne and Annette M. Brodsky. *The Psychology of the Female Offender: A Research Bibliography.* University: University of Alabama, Center for Correctional Psychology, 1976. 45pp. This bibliography was compiled in response to two problems: the general lack of literature on the female offender

and the typical, but incorrect, assumption that what is written about the male offender is also true of his female counterpart. Rosenzweig and Brodsky have brought together works from the correctional, psychological, and sociological literature in order to give as full a picture of the research as possible. No attempt was made to be comprehensive, rather, the editors selected materials for quality and uniqueness. Only works published between 1950 and 1975 were considered. The major portion of the bibliography is divided into sections on the juvenile and the adult offender; each of these is divided into two subcategories: theories, research and treatment. Each subsection is introduced with an informative, brief overview of the major issues and works. A shorter section lists one title each for the crimes women most frequently commit: murder, prostitution, shoplifting, and infanticide; this section also cites articles on women alcoholics and drug addicts. Listings of bibliographies and dissertations conclude the compilation. This interdisciplinary bibliography is an invaluable resource for any researcher concerned with the female offender.

102 Sturgeon, Susan. *Women in Prison: An Annotated Bibliography*. Honolulu: University of Hawaii, Graduate School of Library Studies, 1973. 20pp. Sturgeon originally became interested in this topic as the result of publicity about the case of a local woman. Thus, her perspective is more feminist and ''progressive'' than a disinterested bibliographer's might be. In the introduction, she summarizes some of the key issues surrounding women criminals: the kinds of crimes they commit and why, the discrimination they face, the lack of services. Many of the works cited are from the ''alternative press.'' Organization of the bibliography is by format; it includes sections on dissertations, government documents, and nonprint media as well as the usual books and journal articles. Some of the annotations are not original; sources have been cited in these cases. No materials dated before 1965 are included.

103 —— and Laurel Rans. *The Woman Offender: A Bibliographic Sourcebook*. Pittsburgh: Entropy Limited, 1975. 63pp. The first section of *The Woman Offender* is an annotated listing of 98 citations; an additional 250 citations are listed but not annotated

in the second section. Each of these chapters is subdivided by form of material: books, articles, dissertations. Only literature published in the United States from 1965 to 1975 is included. An appendix lists programs funded by the Department of Labor and the Law Enforcement Assistance Administration.

104   Velimesis, Margaret L. "The Female Offender." *Crime and Delinquency Literature* 7:94–112, March 1974. A bibliographic essay covering the major research on the female offender.

105   *Women Offenders: A Bibliography*. Olympia: Washington State Library, Institutional Library Services, 1970. 14pp. *Supplement*, 1972. 5pp. *Women Offenders* and its *Supplement* are divided into sections by format: books, journal articles, research projects, and special reports. Several works on lesbians are cited, presumably because they touch on prison life and not because homosexuality is regarded as an "offense." Annotations would have been helpful in making this clear. More than half of the works cited are journal articles.

Drugs and Alcohol

The woman alcoholic or drug abuser has long been invisible— isolated in the home, shielded by family and friends. Now that is beginning to change, and a new literature is developing which focuses on her unique problems. The citations listed here were pulled out of the Health section because they were numerous enough to form their own category.

SEE ALSO: Criminal Justice.

106 Beckman, Linda J. "Women Alcoholics: A Review of Social and Psychological Studies." *Journal of Studies of Alcohol* 36:819–824, July 1972.

107 Bowker, Lee H. "An Introduction and Bibliographical Guide to the Literature on Female Drug Use." *Women Studies Abstracts* 5(4):1–18, Winter 1976.

108 Christenson, Susan J. and Alice Q. Swanson. "Women and Drug Use: An Annotated Bibliography." *Journal of Psychedelic Drugs* 6(4):371–414, October/December 1974. Christenson and Swanson address the fact that women have been the world's major drug users, now and historically. The bibliography includes sections on alcohol, psychotherapeutic drugs, narcotics, smoking, and treatment. It is well annotated, and the introduction reviews the major trends and works.

109 Hargraves, Ruth and Muriel Nellis. *Women and Drug Concerns Bibliography*. Washington: United Methodist Church, Board of Church and Society, Department of Drug and Alcohol Concerns, 1974. 9pp.

110 National Institute on Drug Abuse, Clearinghouse for Drug Abuse Information. *Women and Drugs: An Annotated Bibliography*. Rockville, 1975. 62pp. *Women and Drugs* was originally compiled in 1974 by the Student Association for the Study of Hallucinogens. In updating and expanding the bibliography, the Clearinghouse searched a dozen data bases and indexes for literature published between 1937 and 1965. The literature cited is almost exclusively reports of research studies of various

sorts—psychological, physiological, sociological. Each entry is annotated, describing the research in some detail. The 181 citations are categorized into four major chapters: General, Women and Narcotics, Women and Psychotherapeutic Drug Use, Women and Alcohol; each of these is subdivided. There is an author index.

Economics

The Economics section has developed largely during the five years since New Feminist Scholarship was originally compiled. The bibliographies listed here are focused primarily on the status of women in the American economy and, to a lesser extent, the rest of the Western world. Those bibliographies concerned with women's status and role in the economy of developing countries were numerous enough to form a separate section.

SEE ALSO: **Women and Development; Work.**

111 Chapman, Jane Roberts. "Review Essay: Economics." *Signs* 1(1):139–146, Autumn 1975.

112 Dupont, Julie A. *Women—Their Social and Economic Status. Selected References.* Washington: U.S. Department of Labor Library, 1970. 41pp. This selective list includes an interesting array of publications dating from the late nineteenth century through current (as of 1970) titles. It contains many standards and a number of more unusual items from earlier periods. Arranged by subject into eleven categories, it has as well, sections on the origin and function of the Women's Bureau and a listing of special collections on women.

113 Jusenius, Carol L. "Review Essay: Economics." *Signs* 2(1):177–189, Autumn 1976.

114 Kahne, Hilda and Andrew I. Kohen. "Economic Perspective on the Roles of Women in the American Economy." *Journal of Economic Literature* 13:1240–1292, December 1975. This literature review discusses and lists 267 citations to the research on women's economic roles.

115 Kohen, Andrew I., Susan C. Breinich, and Patricia Shields. *Women and the Economy: A Bibliography and Review of the Literature on Sex Differentiation in the Labor Market* and *Supplement.* Columbus: Ohio State University, Center for Human Resource Research, 1977. 109pp. *Women and the Economy* was first issued in 1975. Because of the substantial volume of the literature, it quickly became necessary to update

the bibliography section of the original compilation. Instead of producing a new second edition, however, the first edition was reprinted with a twenty-page supplement. Both the original bibliography and the supplement are classified by subject divisions: Historical Perspective, Female Labor Supply, Earnings, Occupations, Unemployment, Attitudes of and toward Working Women, The Law, Home Production and Child Care, and Studies on the Role of Women. Two final sections complete the bibliography: Bibliographies and Review Articles, Late Arrivals. The Occupations section is further subdivided into more than a dozen categories. The bibliography is comprehensive for research on women's economic roles, but some related areas have been omitted entirely. These include discrimination in education, statistics, and sex differences in occupational choice. Together, the bibliography and its supplement total approximately six hundred citations. The literature review, which is thirty-two pages in length, has not been revised.

116   Lloyd, Cynthia B. "The Role of Women in Modern Economic Life: A Working Bibliography." *Review of Radical Political Economics* 4:121–129, July 1972.

117   Rupen, Alice, Candace Waid, and Leslie Brown. *Women and Credit: An Annotated Bibliography.* Washington: Center for Women Policy Studies, 1974. 27pp. Out of print.

118   Sutton, Ottie K. *Women and the American Economy.* Colorado Springs: U.S. Air Force Academy Library, 1976. 31pp. (Order number: ADA 020334). Sutton's bibliography, representing only a part of the library's holdings on the subject, was prepared in 1976 for an Air Force Academy Assembly on Women and the American Economy. It has seven subject chapters: Reference and Bibliography, History, Discrimination and Equal Rights, Employment and the Family, Labor Force Participation, Occupations, Present Status and Future Role. Each section includes a substantial listing of government documents.

Education

The field of women's education has seen a great deal of activity since 1970: two pieces of major legislation were passed—Title IX and the Women's Educational Equity Act (WEEA); women's studies has blossomed into a full-fledged disciplinary area; women are beginning to enter the male bastions of law and medical school; for the first time, there are more women undergraduates than men. One-third of the bibliographies listed here concern women and higher education. Another third encompass the general area of careers, vocational education, and the relationship of schooling to work as that affects women. Continuing education and equal educational opportunity are each represented by several compilations.

119 Association of Collegiate Alumnae. *Contributions toward a Bibliography of the Higher Education of Women.* Boston: Trustees of the Public Library, 1897. 42pp. Out of print.

120 Astin, Helen S., Nancy Suniewick, and Susan Dweck. *Women: A Bibliography on their Education and Careers.* New York: Behavioral Publications, 1974. 243pp. For the most part, this bibliography covers research materials from the last decade, though some items from the 1950s are included. The citations are arranged by subject into seven chapters, plus one for miscellaneous listings, and two introductory chapters—"Overview of the Findings" and "Beyond the Findings." Entries are annotated or abstracted, and there are author and subject indexes.

121 Barabas, Jean. *Women: Their Education and Career Goals: An Annotated Bibliography of Selected ERIC References.* ERIC, 1972. 71pp. (ED 067 423).

122 Business and Professional Women's Foundation. *Career Counseling: New Perspectives for Women and Girls.* Washington, 1972. 44pp. Out of print. This selected, annotated bibliography is divided into two sections: the first covers materials on research into counseling and occupational choice; the second, specific careers, where to find them, and how to get a job. The

annotations are nonevaluative. Included are books, pamphlets, reports, theses, articles, and microfilm; all are in the collection of the Foundation Library.

123   Cismaresco, Francoise. "Education and Training of Women." *Educational Documentation and Information* 196:14–43, 1975.

124   Froschl, Merle and Jane Williamson. *Feminist Resources for Schools and Colleges: A Guide to Curricular Materials.* 2d rev. ed. Old Westbury: The Feminist Press, 1977. 67pp. The second edition of *Feminist Resources* completely updates the first and also introduces many changes of organization. It lists nonsexist curricular materials for all levels of education as well as many readings on a wide range of relevant issues. (Original edition: Ahlum, Carol and Jacqueline M. Fralley. *Feminist Resources for Schools and Colleges: A Guide to Curricular Materials.* Old Westbury: The Feminist Press, 1973. 20pp.)

125   Harmon, Linda A. *Status of Women in Higher Education: 1963–1972, A Selective Bibliography.* Ames: Iowa State University Library, 1972. 124pp. Covering U.S. materials only, the citations are arranged alphabetically by author and divided into chapters according to type of material covered—books, articles, government publications, dissertations, ERIC, and ephemera. There is no index. An appendix lists civil rights legislation on education and other pertinent laws.

126   Kilson, Marion. "Review Essay: The Status of Women in Higher Education." *Signs* 1(4):935–942, Summer 1976.

127   Lee, Sylvia et al. *Implications of Women's Work Patterns for Vocational and Technical Education; An Annotated Bibliography.* Columbus: Ohio State University, Center for Vocational and Technical Education, 1967. 25pp. This bibliography is one part of a larger project studying the effects of girls' vocational education on their future work lives. While it is now somewhat out of date, it includes material that remains useful. One is encouraged by the early concern of the specialists in home economics education who designed the project.

128 Mills, Gladys H. *Bibliography: Equal Educational Opportunity: Myth or Reality?* ERIC, 1974. 41pp. (ED 110 538). This paper was prepared for the annual meeting of the Education Commission of the States.

129 ———. *Equal Rights for Women in Education.* Denver: Education Commission of the States, 1973. 14pp.

130 Oltman, Ruth M. *Status of Graduate and Professional Education of Women—1974; A Review of the Literature and Bibliography.* ERIC, 1974. 15pp. (ED 092 022). This paper was prepared for the American Association of University Women Conference on Graduate and Professional Education of Women in 1974.

131 Rader, Hannelore B. *Women in Higher Education Administration: Annotated Bibliography.* Washington: National Association for Women Deans, Administrators and Counselors, 1976. 8pp. Primarily, Rader's bibliography covers the period from 1969 to 1975, though a few older items of particular interest have been included. Many of the works cited are studies of the woman administrator, describing her status, the special problems she faces, etc.

132 Robinson, Lora H. *Institutional Analysis of Sex Discrimination: A Review and Annotated Bibliography.* Washington: ERIC Clearinghouse on Higher Education, 1973. 10pp. (ED 076 176).

133 Roby, Pamela. "Women and American Higher Education." *Annals of the American Academy of Political and Social Science* 404:118–139, November 1972.

134 Spiegel, Jeanne. *Continuing Education for Women: A Selected Annotated Bibliography.* Washington: Business and Professional Women's Foundation, 1967. 17pp. Out of print.

135 Watermulder, Georgia P. *Careers for College Women: A Bibliography of Vocational Materials.* Ann Arbor: University of Michigan, Center for Continuing Education for Women, 1968. 61pp. Out of print.

136   Westervelt, Esther Manning. *Barriers to Women's Participation in Postsecondary Education. A Review of Research and Commentary as of 1973-74.* Washington: National Center for Educational Statistics, 1976. 76pp.

137   —— and Deborah Fixter. *Women's Higher and Continuing Education, An Annotated Bibliography.* New York: College Entrance Examination Board, 1971. 67pp. The primary focus of this list is women's higher and continuing education, with secondary emphasis on women's employment. The bibliography is highly selective, yet it covers a broad spectrum of materials. The items were chosen for quality, representativeness, and timeliness; an effort was made to include items that are not easily available. There is no index, and no foreign language materials are included.

138   Women's Educational Equity Communications Network. Operated for the U.S. Office of Education by Far West Laboratory, the Women's Educational Equity Communications Network (WEECN) is ''an information service that collects, screens, classifies, stores, and provides information on projects, activities, and research related to women's educational equity.'' WEECN, funded under the auspices of the Women's Educational Equity Act, was established in 1977. Its mission is to provide a comprehensive information service for a wide diversity of users including teachers, administrators, counselors, students, librarians, and parents. In addition to responding to individual requests, WEECN has developed a publications program including a number of bibliographies. Titles currently in print include:

Cirksena, Kathy et al. *Women's Educational Equity: Annotated Selected References and Resources.* 1977. 16pp.

——. *Continuing Education: Reentry and the Mature Woman, Annotated Selected References and Resources.* 1977. 20pp.

Costick, Rita M. et al. *Nonsexist Career Counseling for Women: Annotated Selected References and Resources.* Part I and II.1978. 23 and 33pp.

Health and Physical Education

In addition to those on women's health concerns in general, this section includes bibliographies on abortion, industrial health and safety, physical education and sports. For general or introductory research, Cowan's Women's Health Care and Ruzek's Women and Health Care are two excellent sources.

SEE ALSO: Drugs and Alcohol; Women and Development.

139 Adams, David. *Therapeutic Abortion: An Annotated Bibliography*. Hamilton: McMaster University Medical Centre, 1973. 98pp.

140 Cowan, Belita. *Women's Health Care: Resources, Writings, Bibliographies*. Ann Arbor: Anshen Publishing, 1977. 52pp. *Women's Health Care* is a model of what a subject bibliography from the women's movement should be: helpful, concise, thoroughly researched, frankly feminist, attractively produced, and modestly priced. It covers the full range of issues in women's health care: Gynecological Self-Help; Sterilization Abuse; Questions and Answers on Menopause; Synthetic Estrogens, DES, and Cancer; Women and Psychotherapy; and includes a brief introductory essay on each. A final section lists recommended feminist periodicals and films. There is a directory of women's health organizations. This bibliography is a must.

141 Dollen, Charles. *Abortion in Context: A Select Bibliography*. Metuchen: Scarecrow Press, 1970. 150pp. This compilation lists "books and articles in the English language that are reasonably available to American scholars and libraries," with emphasis on recent material. "In context" means that articles on related issues such as marriage, family, and contraception have been included. Dollen concentrates on the moral and philosophical side of the abortion issue and leaves the medical literature out. There is a subject and source index.

142 Floyd, Mary K. *Abortion Bibliography*. Troy: Whitson, Vol. I–VI, 1970–1975. The *Abortion Bibliography* annually lists

books and articles as a "contribution toward documenting in one place as comprehensively as possible one of our central social issues." The bibliography includes an unannotated list of books, alphabetically listed by author; and periodical literature in two sections, one by title and one by subject. Foreign material seems to be well covered. There is an author index.

143   Geijerstom, Gunnar K. *An Annotated Bibliography of Induced Abortion.* Ann Arbor: University of Michigan, Center for Population Planning, 1969. 359pp.

144   Glab, Kathi. "Sporting Women." *Booklegger* 6:9–12, September/October 1974. Lamenting the lack of resources on and for sportswomen, Glab gives a selected list of the books and periodicals that do exist. She also includes a comprehensive list of associations for women in various sports. As this bibliography is now somewhat out-of-date, there are many new works available.

145   Henriques, Cynthia. *Women in Health: An Annotated Bibliography.* Chicago, n.d. 17pp. (Order from Pauline Bart). The works cited in this bibliography are primarily on the female health-care worker; there are sections on women physicians, dentists, and nurses as well as the nurse-doctor relationship. There are two brief sections on the woman as health-care consumer, one focusing on the sex stereotyping found in mental health care. Unfortunately, half the bibliography is a listing of the reference sources consulted, and selected annotations of these sources. The annotations tend to point out the overall dearth of material published on women health-care workers. The bibliography covers the period from 1970 to 1973.

146   Hunt, Vilma R. *The Health of Women at Work.* Evanston: Northwestern University, The Program on Women, 1977. 173pp. Hunt's compilation is a hefty and impressive one. She has organized her material into seventeen categories, thirteen of which relate to the type of health problem under study—accidents, noise, radiation, toxic substances, etc. The other four sections are: History of Working Women, Occupational Health Serivces, U.S. Government (documents), International Labor Office (documents). Most of the medical literature cited is

recent—since 1970—while the history and government documents sections include sources from the turn of the century forward. Each section is divided into English and foreign language segments, with the foreign language half considerably the larger in many instances. Each of the major divisions has a brief introduction describing the scope and content of the literature. An excellent source.

147 Kennard, June A. "Review Essay: The History of Physical Education." *Signs* 2(4):835–842, Summer 1977.

148 National Association for Women and Girls in Sport, Research Committee. *Bibliography of Research Involving Female Subjects: A Compilation of Theses and Dissertations in Physical Education, Health and Recreation.* Washington: American Alliance for Health, Physical Education and Recreation, 1974. 205pp.

149 Ruzek, Sheryl K. *Women and Health Care: A Bibliography with Selected Annotation.* Joint publication of the Institute for Scientific Analysis and Northwestern University, The Program on Women, 1975. 76pp. (Order from Northwestern University). This bibliography covers a wide range of health concerns relating to women. The first section, Women's Health Care—Feminist Perspective, is annotated and gives a good introduction to a feminist idea of women's health. Rape and industrial health/safety are not covered and the professional medical literature was not reviewed for inclusion.

150 U.S. Department of Labor, Women's Bureau. *Selected References on the Health of Women in Industry.* Washington, 1929. 8pp. Out of print. This bibliography consists largely of government documents; it is divided into one general category and then various categories according to the industry or health problem considered.

History

Nearly half the bibliographies in this section concentrate on American women's history; remaining entries have a focus on European history from Antiquity through the twentieth century. Three bibliographies are concerned with women's role in the two world wars, and there are two entries on women in revolution—Cuban and Russian.

SEE ALSO: General; Third-World Countries; Women's Movement.

151 Arthur, Marilyn B. "Review Essay: Classics." *Signs* 2(2):382–403, Winter 1976.

152 Business and Professional Women's Foundation. *Women and Work in U.S. History*. Washington, 1976. 28pp. This pamphlet is an excellent basic bibliography. The brief "Overview of Resources" summarizes nicely the major aspects of women's work history. The bibliography itself is in four parts: Methods and Theory in Women's History; Earlier Scholarship; Contemporary Scholarship (document collections, books, and journals); and Guides to Further Resources. Each entry is carefully annotated. There is an author index.

153 The Common Women Collective. *Women in U.S. History: An Annotated Bibliography*. Cambridge, 1976. 114p. *Women in U.S. History* is a useful, though uneven, bibliography. Some of the subject categorizing seems a bit quirky, but that will always be the case and those oddities that do exist are covered by cross-references. There is also some unevenness in the depth of coverage. For example, the temperance section has only six entries, all of which are biographies of only two women: Frances Willard and Carry Nation. This, despite the quantity of scholarship in the field. Contrast that with the section on nineteenth and twentieth century sexuality, a relatively new field. Its thirty-eight entries comprise a very high proportion of the total work available. The bibliography is divided into twenty-four short sections by form of work, topic, or period and is cross-referenced such that the lack of an index is not problematical. The annotations are informative and evaluative. Criteria used in evaluating the works include feminist perspective, social and

economic class consciousness, inclusion of traditionally omitted groups, writing style, documentation, and availability. Each of these criteria is discussed and explained in the introduction. Entries which are particularly suited to high school readers are marked with an asterisk.

154 Davis, Natalie Zemon and Jill K. Conway. *Society and the Sexes: A Bibliography of Women's History in Early Modern Europe, Colonial America, and the United States.* New York: Garland, forthcoming.

155 Erickson, Carolly and Kathleen Casey. "Women in the Middle Ages: A Working Bibliography." *Medieval Studies* 37:340–359, 1975.

156 Fox, Vicki G. "The Role of Women in the American Revolution: An Annotated Bibliography." *Indiana Social Studies Quarterly* 28:14–29, Spring 1975.

157 Goodwater, Leanna. *Women in Antiquity: An Annotated Bibliography.* Metuchen: Scarecrow Press, 1975. 171pp. This bibliography, intended for use in an academic library, covers women in Greece and Rome from the earliest records until 476 A.D. Biographies make up the bulk of the book, with Sappho and Cleopatra excluded because of the amount of material on both. Literary and textual criticism is also excluded. The list is in two parts: Ancient Sources and Modern Works. The modern section includes materials published since 1872; it attempts to be comprehensive for English language materials and selective in foreign languages. The introduction is a general discussion of women in antiquity.

158 Graham, Patricia Alberg. "So Much to Do: Guides for Historical Research on Women in Higher Education." *Teachers College Record* 76(3):412–429, February 1975.

159 Greco, Norma and Ronaele Novotny. "Bibliography of Women in the English Renaissance." *University of Michigan Papers in Women's Studies* 1:30–57, June 1974.

160   Horne, Grenda. "The Liberation of British and American Women's History." *Bulletin of the Society for the Study of Labor History* 26:28–39, 1973.

161   Kanner, S. Barbara. *Women in English Society, 1066–1945: Interpretive and Bibliographical Essays.* London: Archon Books, forthcoming.

162   Kelly, Joan. *Bibliography in the History of European Women.* 4th rev. ed. Bronxville: Sarah Lawrence College, Women's Studies Program, 1976. 132pp. Kelly's "working bibliography," first compiled for her students at Sarah Lawrence College, has grown beyond that over the years. Arranged according to standard historical periods, it covers the history of European women from Antiquity to World War II. In addition to the chronological sections, there is a general section on the history of women, one on historiography, and one on reference materials. The coverage is broad, including, for example, literary studies, autobiography and biography. Primary sources are marked with an asterisk. (Original edition: Kelly-Gadol, Joan. *Women's History: A Critically Selected Bibliography.* Bronxville: Sarah Lawrence College, Women's Studies Program, n.d. 54pp.)

163   Leonard, Eugenie A., Sophie H. Drinker, and Miriam Y. Holden. *The American Woman in Colonial and Revolutionary Times, 1565–1800.* Philadelphia: University of Pennsylvania Press, 1962. Reprint. Westport: Greenwood Press, 1974. 169pp. Originally published in 1962 by the University of Pennsylvania Press, *The American Woman in Colonial and Revolutionary Times* has been reprinted by Greenwood in a facsimile edition. The first section of the book is a detailed syllabus in outline form for a complete study of the woman in the earliest period of American history, from 1565 to 1800. In relation to the bibliography, the syllabus acts as a subject organizer. It has ten major divisions, with titles such as Women in Earliest Settlements, The Status and Rights of Colonial Women, Woman's Domain—The Home, and Colonial Women in the Productive Life of the Communities. Each of these is subdivided by topic or

geography through several levels. For example, Woman's Domain—the Home is subdivided as follows: 2. Women as Wives in the Colonial Home; A. Marriages; a. Courtship and Early Marriage. Abbreviated citations are listed under each of the syllabus divisions; full bibliographic information for the more than one thousand works is found in the bibliography section, a straight alphabetical listing. A third section is designed to aid the researcher of individual women. Each entry in this section lists the name, home, birth/death dates, husband's name, and significant contribution of "104 Outstanding Colonial Women." This compilation does not suffer from the usual class and nationalist bias that defines "colonial" as English and free. A clear effort has been made to include information on the Spanish settlements of the Southwest, women of every nationality and religious group, and those who came in bondage as well as in freedom. The only serious flaw of this volume is that it has not been updated since 1962.

164 Lerner, Gerda. *Bibliography in the History of American Women.* 3d ed. Bronxville: Sarah Lawrence College, Women's Studies Program, 1978. 79pp. Gerda Lerner tells us in her introduction that this third edition of her bibliography will be the last, since the volume of new material would make any future compilation book-length. She takes an interdisciplinary approach, arranging the bibliography into fourteen subject chapters from Historiography to Sexuality, Family History to Women and Art. The single largest section, History of American Women, is twenty-one pages long (about one-fourth of the whole) and is divided into eleven subcategories. In all, there are more than one thousand citations making this one of the most comprehensive sources for the history of American women. (Original edition: Lerner, Gerda. *Women's Studies: History of Women in America.* Bronxville: Sarah Lawrence College, Women's Studies Program, 1972. 41pp.)

165 Loader, Joyce. "Women in the Left, 1906–1941: Bibliography of Primary Sources." *University of Michigan Papers in Women's Studies* 2(1):9–82, September 1975. This bibliography has as its primary focus works on women written by women of the left. It is

in three major sections: Anarchism; The Literary Left; The Communist Party (1920–1941), which is by far the largest. There is an index to names.

166   Lougee, Carolyn C. "Review Essay: Modern European History." *Signs* 2(3):628–650, Spring 1977.

167   Palmegiano, E.M. *Women and British Periodicals*. New York: Garland, 1976. 118pp. This interesting bibliography covers material about women in the periodical press in England from 1832 to 1867. The dates were chosen because they mark, roughly, a time often ignored in Victorian women's history—the era between Wolstonecraft and Mill when women were *most* regarded as nonpersons. The bibliography section is in two parts: the first, a checklist of British women's periodicals; the second, a checklist of articles on women in British periodicals. Libraries with most complete holdings are included in the first list. In addition to this bibliographic work, there is a series of essays on the different images of women found in the periodicals listed: The Ladies, Milkhands and Maids, Domestic Economists, The Redundant, The Magdalens, The Emancipated, and The Lords of Creation. An invaluable reference for anyone doing work in the period.

168   Perez, Louis A. "Women in the Cuban Revolutionary War, 1953–58: A Bibliography." *Science and Society* 39:104–108, Spring 1975.

169   Pomeroy, Sarah B. "Selected Bibliography on Women in Antiquity." *Arethusa* 6(1):125–157, Spring 1973. This is a bibliographic essay with a suggested syllabus for an undergraduate class on women in Classical Antiquity.

170   Sicherman, Barbara. "Review Essay: American History." *Signs* 1(2):461–486, Winter 1975.

171   U.S. Council of National Defense, Woman Committee. *Woman in the War, A Bibliography*. Washington, 1918. Out of print.

172 U.S. Library of Congress. *Brief List of References on Women in the Russian Revolution.* Washington, 1918. Out of print.

173 ———. *List of References on Women's Work in the European War.* Washington, 1918. Out of print.

174 ———. *Select List of References on Women in Colonial Days.* Washington, 1913. Out of print.

175 ———. *Woman's Part of World War II, A List of References.* Washington, 1942. Out of print.

176 Verbrugge, Martha H. "Review Essay: Women and Medicine in Nineteenth-Century America." *Signs* 1(4):957–972, Summer 1976.

Law

The Equal Rights Amendment is a major legal issue which connects the two waves of the women's movement: it was born out of the first wave and is being pursued by the second. There are bibliographies on the ERA from both periods in this section, though the latter compilation is comprehensive enough to supersede the former. Other, general bibliographies on women's legal status complete the section.

SEE ALSO: **Work.**

177 Babcock, Barbara et al. *Women and the Law: A Collection of Reading Lists.* Pittsburgh: KNOW, 1971. 31pp. Included in the collection is a course outline for a basic women and the law course and the reading lists for each section as compiled by teachers.

178 Equal Rights Amendment Project. *The Equal Rights Amendment: A Bibliographic Study.* Westport: Greenwood Press, 1976. 367pp. This is a comprehensive work (almost six thousand entries) citing nearly every word written about the ERA since its inception in 1921. The volume is organized into chapters by form of media since the "overlapping of subjects make a topical arrangement haphazard at best." The major sections are Congressional Publications; Other Government Documents; Books and Dissertations; Pamphlets; Brochures and Papers; Periodical Material (legal and academic journals, newsletters, and newspapers). There is a separate section under "Periodical Material" for *Equal Rights* (1923–1954), the organ of the National Woman's Party, which gives the most detailed history of the ERA for that period. It is arranged chronologically as are the newspaper sections. Overall, the volume includes three types of material: "reportage, which serves an historical function; argumentation, which defines the controversy; and analysis of the specifically legal effects of the amendment." The introduction provides a good brief history of the ERA as well as an overview of the major issues.

179 Hughes, Marija Matich. "Women's Rights: A Selected Bibliography." *International Journal of Law Literature* 4(3):216–248, November 1976.

180   U.S. Library of Congress. *Brief List of References on the Rights of Women.* Washington, 1922. Out of print.

181   ———. *List of References on the Equal Rights Amendment Proposed by National Woman's Party.* Washington, 1923. Out of print.

182   ———. *List of References on the Legal Status of Women.* Washington, 1914. Out of print.

Lesbians

Three of the four bibliographies listed here primarily are guides to lesbian themes in literature; they do not include research or other, general nonfiction. Taken together, they provide comprehensive access to the genre. A Gay Bibliography from the American Library Association's Gay Task Force is the one bibliography restricted to nonfiction.

183 American Library Association, SRRT Task Force on Gay Liberation. *A Gay Bibliography.* 5th ed. Philadelphia, 1975. 8pp. *Supplement,* 1976. 2pp. The SRRT (Social Responsibilities Round Table) Gay Task Force, formed in 1970, was the first such caucus of a professional association to form. The Task Force has been involved in many activities since then, only one of which is the compilation and distribution of this bibliography. The 250 entries are organized according to format and are not annotated. The bibliography is exclusively nonfiction, listing only those works which present a positive view of homosexuality, have some historical value, or help the reader to understand the gay experience. A sixth edition will be available in the summer of 1979.

184 Damon, Gene, Jan Watson, and Robin Jordan. *The Lesbian in Literature: A Bibliography.* 2d ed. Reno: The Ladder, 1975. 96pp. The size of this bibliography/pamphlet is deceptive; it looks small, but packs an incredible amount of information into its ninety-six pages. The bibliography consists almost totally of English language fiction (including novels, short stories, poetry, drama and fictionalized biography), though recent (post 1967) unprejudiced nonfiction is also included. The cut-off date is copyright 1974. Each entry is rated on two scales: primacy of lesbian character/plot and quality of lesbian material. A third symbol, ''T,'' denotes literature that is essentially trash. However, in keeping with the changing consciousness of and about lesbians, most T-rated books (three thousand!) have been deleted from this second edition. Title changes, literary form, and binding are also indicated. Invaluable for any and all readers/researchers of lesbian literature. (Original edition: Damon, Gene and Lee Stuart. *Lesbians in Literature: A Bibliography.* San Francisco: Daughters of Bilitis, 1967.)

185 *A Gay Bibliography: Eight Bibliographies on Lesbian and Male Homosexuality.* New York: Arno Press, 1975. This compilation is one volume of a reprint series on homosexuality. Eight pioneering bibliographies of lesbian and male homosexual literature published between 1958 and 1966 have been rescued from obscurity and bound together in a form libraries can easily procure. The eight are: *Astra's Tower: Special Leaflet #2* and *#3* by Marion Bradley Zimmer; *Checklist 1960, Checklist Supplement 1961* and *1962* by Marion Bradley Zimmer and Gene Damon; *The Lesbian in Literature: A Bibliography* by Gene Damon and Lee Stuart; *The Homosexual in Literature: A Chronological Bibliography Circa 700 B.C.–1958* by Noel I. Garde; and *Homosexuality: Selected Abstracts and Bibliography* by Wiliam Parker.

186 Kuda, Marie J. *Women Loving Women: A Select and Annotated Bibliography of Women Loving Women in Literature.* Chicago: Womanpress, 1975. 28pp. This bibliography was first published by Lavender Press in 1974; for its second printing, the identical text was published by Womanpress in 1975. The works cited are limited to English language fiction, poetry, biography and autobiography. An effort was made to include works which "show lesbianism as a valid, positive and alternative lifestyle," as well as prototypical works—the first of any genre that was eventually widely copied (student/teacher, governesses, prison or army milieu, etc.). The annotations are informative and well-written.

Life Cycles

One hears a great deal today about "women in transition." While this section focuses on transition issues, "Life Cycles" seemed to be a more descriptive title. Older women have been active for several years now working against the double discrimination of age and sex, and a substantial body of literature has been produced in the process. There are separate bibliographies on two key issues of concern to older women: widowhood and menopause. At the other end of the age spectrum, the resources are scarce. Efforts to apply the thinking and lessons of feminism to the special problems of adolescent girls and young women is still relatively new, but this is a fast developing program area. While there is only one bibliography listed here, a more substantial literature will undoubtedly follow.

187 *Annotated Bibliography, 1964-1974, of the Needs, Concerns and Aspirations of Adolescent Girls, 12-18 Years.* St. Paul: University of Minnesota, Center for Youth Development and Research, 1975. 204pp. Out of print. This bibliography is the result of a thorough literature search of writings since 1964 on seventeen aspects of the adolescent girl's life, including education, family, friends, and sexuality. The compilation also includes the bibliography from Gisela Konopka's book *Young Girls: A Portrait of Adolescence,* which is a section unto itself and is organized differently from the rest of the bibliography. The other chapters are arranged according to the source indexed: *American Book Publishing Record, Crime and Delinquency Abstracts,* ERIC, Medline, *Psychological Abstracts* and Helen Astin's *Women's Higher and Continuing Education.* There are two final sections, one on dissertations and the other miscellaneous.

188 Barrett, Carol J. "Review Essay: Women in Widowhood." *Signs* 2(4):856–868, Summer 1977.

189 Interface Bibliographers. *Age Is Becoming: An Annotated Bibliography on Women and Aging.* Oakland: National Organization of Women, Task Force on Older Women, 1976. 35pp. (Order from Glide Publications). The NOW Task Force on Older Women commissioned this bibliography to help them deal with

an ever-increasing volume of information requests. It is a selective compilation of works on women in the "post-parental" period, published between 1970 and 1975. Both scholarly and general works are included. There are subject sections on women re-entering the job/education market, role changes, financial difficulties, sexuality, medical/physical developments, and widowhood, and one of biographies. *Age Is Becoming* provides access to the literature of an emerging field and should prove useful to a wide variety of collections.

190   Seidlitz, Sarah. *The Menopause: A Selective Bibliography*. Oakland: National Organization of Women, Task Force on Older Women, 1976. 7pp. Out of print.

191   Strugnell, Cecile. *Adjustment to Widowhood and Some Related Problems: A Selected and Annotated Bibliography*. New York: Health Sciences Publishing, 1974. 201pp. This bibliography is limited to books and articles published since 1972.

Literature

Despite the fact that literature was one of the first fields to be influenced by women's studies, the bibliographies have been slow to appear—most of them since 1974. An early attempt (1971) was made by women in the Modern Language Association, but it was not maintained. The bibliography of women writers first produced in 1973 by the Sense and Sensibility Collective (now the Women and Literature Collective) has received fairly wide distribution; it has been the major source on literature by women. Several compilations on literary criticism—feminist and otherwise—have appeared in recent years. Women and Literature, the quarterly journal, is now providing an ongoing bibliography in a special edition of the fall issue each year. There is one bibliography of drama by women.

SEE ALSO: Lesbians.

192 Backscheider, Paula R., Felicity Nussbaum, and Philip B. Anderson. *An Annotated Bibliography of Twentieth-Century Critical Studies of Women and Literature, 1660–1800.* New York: Garland, 1977. 287pp. This bibliography actually covers a somewhat broader field than the title suggests. It includes "critical and scholarly books and articles published between 1900 and 1975" on women—not just literary women, though they are undoubtedly featured. The compilers had researchers of the Restoration and the eighteenth century in mind as well as the women's studies researcher. The first major section of the volume is devoted to general studies of the period, including literary criticism, social history, biography, and art history. The second section is restricted to works on literature and is divided by genre. It also includes information on six major male novelists (Cleland, Defoe, Fielding, Richardson, Smollett, Sterne), listing critical studies of their female characters and works describing their influence on and relationships to women and women writers. The final and largest section (approximately two-thirds of the more than 1,500 entries) lists various works of sixty-five women writers of the period, from Mary Astell to Ann Yearsley. There is an index to Restoration and eighteenth-century women, and an index to authors.

193   Batchelder, Eleanor. *Plays by Women: A Bibliography*. New York: Womanbooks, 1977. 41pp. This was the only drama bibliography I could locate, and it fills an important gap. A rough count indicates the inclusion of approximately 150 playwrights who are listed alphabetically, followed by a chronological roster of plays. Plays appearing in anthologies receive an abbreviated entry, with full information in the anthologies section at the back. Each anthology entry gives the complete contents. For the most part, authors are twentieth-century American playwrights. This small pamphlet contains a gold-mine of information and should be a very welcome addition.

194   Boos, Florence. "1974 Bibliography of Women in British and American Literature: 1660–1900." *Women and Literature* 3(2):33–64, Fall 1975. This is the first of an annual bibliography indexing nearly two hundred scholarly journals. It lists all articles about British and American women writers from 1660 to 1900. The bibliography is arranged by a unique decimal system in which the period and country of origin are denoted by the number to the left of the decimal and the form of the writing by the number to the right.

195   ———. "1975 Bibliography of Literature in English by and about Women, 600–1960." *Women and Literature* issued as a supplement to vol. 4, no. 2, Fall 1976. 148pp. The second annual issue of this bibliography is considerably different from the first. The number of journals indexed doubled, from about two hundred to approximately four hundred. Both the chronological and geographical coverage were increased; the chronological in two directions (backward to 600 and forward to 1960) and the geographical from just British and American writers to those of all English-speaking countries. These changes produced a dramatic increase in size, and the bibliography had to be issued as a separate supplement. The basic organization of the bibliography remains unchanged.

196   ———. "1976 Bibliography of Literature in English by and about Women, 600–1960." *Women and Literature* issued as a supplement to vol. 5, no. 2., Fall 1977. 168pp. The third annual

volume follows the same format and scope of the second. Because of the enormity of the task and the dependence on volunteer efforts, the 1976 index was not mailed to subscribers until February of 1978. The National Endowment for the Humanities has provided a grant for the bibliography in order to ease some of these problems and assure its continuation.

197 Fries, Maureen and Anne M. Daunis. *A Bibliography of Writings by and about Women Authors, British and American, 1957-1969.* Charleston: Women's Caucus for the Modern Languages, 1971. 73pp. Out of print.

198 Kolodny, Annette. "Review Essay: Literary Criticism." *Signs* 2(2):404–421, Winter 1976.

199 Loventhal, Milton. *Autobiographies of Women, 1946-1970, A Bibliography.* San Jose: California State University Library, 1972. Out of print. A revised, expanded version is in progress as of this writing.

200 Marks, Elaine. "Review Essay: Women and Literature in France." *Signs* 3(4):832–842, Summer 1978.

201 Myers, Carol Fairbanks. *Women in Literature: Criticism of the Seventies.* Metuchen: Scarecrow Press, 1976. 256pp. Fairbanks's bibliography is arranged dictionary-style, with headings for each author from A to Z. Listed under the authors' names are citations to criticism of various sorts, interviews, book reviews, and discussions of female characters. A final, general section lists works that are not confined to one author or character. The bibliography covers the period from January 1970 through spring 1975. There is an index of critics and editors.

202 Nower, Joyce. *Selected Bibliography of Women Writers.* San Diego, 1970. 17pp. (Order from Center for Women's Studies and Services). Nower lists the works of selected women writers of twenty-five countries from Argentina to Uruguay. There is a heading for each country, with the authors listed alphabetically under each except in the case of the United States where there is further subdivision by racial or ethnic group. The citations are

not to specific editions of the authors' works, but rather include only title and date of original publication.

203 Reynolds, Judy. *Women as Authors.* San Jose: San Jose State University Library, 1974. 16pp. This bibliography lists more than 250 citations to books and articles on women writers including novelists, poets, playwrights, journalists. It lists works on the woman writer in general, not on specific authors. Available in limited supply to educational institutions only.

204 ———. *Women in Literature.* San Jose: San Jose State University Library, 1974. 28pp. This bibliography lists more than four hundred citations to books and articles on the image of women in literature. Available in limited supply to educational institutions only.

205 Rosenfelt, Deborah Silverton. *Strong Women: An Annotated Bibliography of Literature for the High School Classroom.* Old Westbury: The Feminist Press, 1976. 56pp. This attractive pamphlet lists more than one hundred annotated citations to works by women writers. The title says the literature cited is for the high school classroom, but the introduction reveals the editor's assumption that "high school readers will enjoy many of the same works that have moved older audiences." Thus, the bibliography will be of equal use to the college teacher or student. The compilation is divided into sections by form (anthologies, autobiography and biography, drama, novels, short stories, poetry) and has a topical index.

206 Schwartz, Narda Lacey. *Articles on Women Writers 1960–1975, A Bibliography.* Santa Barbara: ABC-Clio, 1977. 236pp. Narda Schwartz has compiled an extensive bibliography of articles, both popular and scholarly, on more than six hundred women writers from the English-speaking world. She searched twenty-one bibliographies and literature indexes as well as *Dissertation Abstracts.* Included is any woman writer —and writer is defined broadly to include diarists, essayists, and letter writers, as well as the usual novelists and poets—about whom at least one article appeared between 1960 and 1975. The time frame was chosen to give a record of the changing attitudes about women writers

occasioned by the emergence and growth of the women's movement. The bibliography is arranged dictionary-style, from Hannah Adams to Charlotte Zolotow. Each entry gives the author's name and pseudonym, birth and death dates, and country where most of the writing was done. The author entries have three subdivisions: Bibliography (collections of critical studies); General Works (biographical, thematic, and comparative studies); and Individual Works (the author's primary literature listed by title and followed by the articles on each). This is a fine source which should be of use to a large audience.

207 Showalter, Elaine. "Review Essay: Literary Criticism." *Signs* 1(2):435–460, Winter 1975.

208 U.S. Library of Congress. *List of References on Women in Literature*. Washington, 1922. Out of print.

209 White, Barbara A. *American Women Writers: An Annotated Bibliography of Criticism*. New York: Garland, 1977. 126pp. White's bibliography covers what she calls "criticism in general"—that is, criticism of women writers as a group, not that of specific writers. It includes "published criticism on American women writers of fiction, poetry, and drama" through 1975. The material is arranged into ten chapters: biography; criticism on specific groups; specific topics (genre); literary history; contemporary assessments (contemporaries of the critic, that is, not of the 1970s); feminine sensibility; the problems of women writers; discriminatory treatment of women writers ("Phallic Criticism"); feminist criticism; and miscellaneous. Her introduction provides a brief, interesting overview of the major themes, problems, and assumptions in current and past thinking about women writers. Her conclusions: *Plus ça change, plus c'est la même chose.*

210 Women and Literature Collective. *Women and Literature: An Annotated Bibliography of Women Writers*. 3d ed. Cambridge, 1976. 212pp. Both the collective and the bibliography have changed and grown over the years and through three editions. The third edition is greatly expanded and has been partially revised. While all annotations from the previous editions were

read and reconsidered, they were not all rewritten, thus, there is substantial variety in style and outlook from entry to entry. The more than eight hundred citations are arranged by country and subdivided by chronology. Most of the volume (more than half) is devoted to American and British writers, however, sixteen other countries, continents, or geographical areas are also covered. Listings for major authors include biographical sketches. Not every work of every author is listed; there are inevitable gaps, none of them serious. There is a section for anthologies and one for literary criticism, and a special effort was made to include the publications of the women's presses. There are author and subject indexes. (Original edition: Sense and Sensibility Collective. *Women and Literature: An Annotated Bibliography of Women Writers*. Cambridge, 1973. 58pp.)

Marriage and the Family

New research has made significant changes in the study of Marriage and the Family, which until recently has been the traditional discipline for the study of women. The home no longer enjoys its reputation as a haven of domestic tranquility; it has been exposed as a place of domestic violence. Research on violent husbands and battered women—some of it problematic from a feminist point of view—is enjoying something of a vogue right now. There are three bibliographies on battered women. The general area of marriage and the family is dominated by the comprehensive efforts of the University of Minnesota in its <u>International Bibliography of Research</u>. Divorce is also included in this section, with two listings.

SEE ALSO: Child Care.

211　Howard, Pamela F. *Wife Beating: A Selected Annotated Bibliography*. San Diego: Current Bibliography Series, 1978. 57pp. Compiled primarily for the general public, this bibliography would be of interest as well to the researcher, student, or social work practitioner. It cites a wide range of materials, running the gamut from research studies published in scholarly journals to newspaper articles to "how-to" manuals produced by women's shelters. The citations are organized into sections by format: Books and pamphlets, periodical articles, newspaper articles, newsbank (a newspaper indexing service), government publications, films. The last section is a brief listing of agencies in the United States, Canada, and England from which written material is available; it is not a comprehensive list. The annotations are informative and well-written.

212　*International Bibliography of Research in Marriage and the Family, 1900–1964*. Joan Aldous and Reuben Hill, eds. Minneapolis: University of Minnesota Press, 1967. 508pp. *See #* 215 for annotation.

213　*International Bibliography of Research in Marriage and the Family, Volume II, 1965–1972*. Joan Aldous and Nacy Dahl, eds. Minneapolis: University of Minnesota Press, 1974, 1,530pp. *See #215* for annotation.

214 *Inventory of Marriage and Family Literature, 1973 & 1974, Volume III.* Nancy Dahl and David H. L. Olson, eds. St. Paul: University of Minnesota, Family Social Science, 1975. 376pp. *See* #215 for annotation.

215 *Inventory of Marriage and Family Literature, 1975 & 1976, Volume IV.* Nancy Dahl and David H. L. Olson, eds. St. Paul: University of Minnesota, Family Social Science, 1977. 638pp. This bibliography began in 1967 in an attempt to list every research item in the interdisciplinary area of marriage and the family published since 1900. "Research" was defined broadly to include any work that reports on empirical data. Thus, it is easier to list what was not included: unpublished theses, proscriptive works, studies of the individual in which the focus is not family behavior, population studies which do not relate findings to the family, textbooks, popular works, legal treatises. The literature search resulted in 12,850 citations to books, journal articles, and miscellaneous papers in the first edition. The bibliography was computer-generated and consists of five parts: KWIC (Key-Word-In-Context) Index, Subject index, Complete Reference List, Author Index, and Periodicals List. The regular subject index was included in addition to the KWIC index for the convenience of those unfamiliar with KWIC indexing. Citations were listed alphabetically; foreign titles were translated. The introduction concludes with a literature review describing the trends in research over the years. *Volume II* follows the same format as the first edition. It lists 12,870 citations to research on the family, including titles for the 1900–1964 period which were missed. The third volume represents a change in scope; instead of listing all research published, it is essentially an index to nearly five hundred journals in the interdisciplinary area of marriage and the family. It lists 2,413 citations to articles published in English. *Volume IV* follows the format of *Volume III,* and indexes approximately 750 journals. The editors intend the bibliography to become an annual index, but have not yet been successful.

216 Israel, Stanley. *A Bibliography on Divorce.* New York: Bloch Publishing, 1974. 300pp. Israel's bibliography has sections on

three major aspects of divorce: legal, religious, and sociological. Each entry gives the publisher's address and the complete table of contents of the book in addition to the usual citation information and annotation. Though it is not so explained in the introduction, the annotations do not appear to have been written by Stanley Israel, but rather to be jacket copy or some essentially promotional writing supplied by the publisher. The value of this type of listing is certainly questionable. Approximately 150 books are annotated in this way, comprising the bulk of the book. Additional titles for which full listings could not be provided are cited briefly at the end.

217   Lystad, Mary Henamann. "Violence at Home: A Review of the Literature." *American Journal of Orthopsychiatry* 45:328–345, April 1975.

218   McKenney, Mary. *Divorce: A Selected Annotated Bibliography.* Metuchen: Scarecrow Press, 1975. 157pp. Mary McKenney has listed every "significant" work on divorce written in English and published before 1972 that she was able to locate. A few items of doubtful significance—but of particular interest—are also included, as are all popular and statistical works and a sampling of fiction and films. Her attitude to divorce is solidly feminist and is expressed in the introduction and annotations. The bibliography is arranged by subject into eleven major sections; appendixes list resource organizations and divorce laws state by state. There are author and subject indexes.

219   McShane, Claudette. *Annotated Bibliography on Woman Battering.* Milwaukee: University of Wisconsin, School of Social Welfare, Midwest Parent-Child Welfare Resource Center, 1977. 25pp. This bibliography combines the two major types of literature available on battered women: the professionally-oriented sociological or psychological research studies and the activist-oriented writings of feminists who are trying to provide solutions. The bibliography is arranged by format into five sections: monographs, articles, newsletters, guidebooks, and media. In each section, the annotated entries are followed by a list of citations the editor was not able to review.

Minority and Ethnic Women

This section is dominated by nine bibliographies on black women. This is probably largely due to the emergence of Black Studies as the first of the ethnic studies areas to develop. There are three bibliographies on Spanish-speaking women and one on Native American women. No bibliographies on Asian-American women were found. Of the white ethnic groups, only bibliographies on Jewish women were located.

220 Cabello-Argendona, Roberto, Juan Gomez-Quinones, and Pat Herrera Duran. *The Chicana: A Comprehensive Bibliographic Study*. Los Angeles: University of California, Chicano Studies Center, 1975. 308pp.

221 Cole, Johnetta. "Black Women in America: An Annotated Bibliography." *Black Scholar* 3:42–53, December 1971.

222 Concilio Mujeres. *Bibliography on la Mujer*. San Francisco, 1974. 12pp. Out of print. Compiled by a Chicana women's rights group, the bibliography includes articles, papers, films, photos, resources, and additional information on Chicana and other Spanish-speaking women. The compilers are at work on a new edition.

223 Davis, Lenwood G. *The Black Woman in American Society: A Selected Annotated Bibliography*. Boston: G. K. Hall, 1975. 159pp. Davis's bibliography includes approximately seven hundred citations to books, articles, pamphlets, and government documents on the American black woman. The citations are arranged by format, with only the books and articles sections annotated. In addition to the chapters of actual bibliography, there are listings of relevant library collections, organizations, black women newspaper editors/publishers and elected officials, and population statistics.

224 ———. *Black Women in the Cities, 1872-1973; A Bibliography of Published Works on the Life and Achievements of Black Women in Cities in the United States*. 2d ed. Monticello: Council of Planning Librarians, 1975. 75pp. The second edition

of this bibliography is approximately fifty percent longer than the first. In the main bibliography section, it includes more than five hundred citations to books, articles, pamphlets, reports, and government documents on the urban black woman. In addition, there are sections on general reference works, selected black journals, libraries with special collections on black history, journals on urban affairs, related Council bibliographies, black women's national organizations and black women elected officials. Several of these sections also appear in Davis's 1975 bibliography, *The Black Woman in American Society* (#223), so there is some duplication. The bibliography is arranged by format, which may cause difficulties as there is no subject index. Arrangement by broad subjects such as housing, unemployment, divorce, welfare, or education might have been more useful. The materials range widely and cover urban problems generally as much as they do the urban black woman. Davis's bibliography is a starting point for the sociologist, urban planner, or historian. (Original edition: Davis, Lenwood G. *Black Women in the Cities 1872-1972: A Bibliography of Published Works on the Life and Achievements of Black Women in Cities in the United States.* Monticello: Council of Planning Librarians, 1972.)

225 "The Jewish Woman: A Selected Bibliography." *Response* 7:183–187, Summer 1973.

226 Klotman, Phyllis R. and Wilmer H. Baatz. *The Black Family and the Black Woman: A Bibliography.* 2d ed. New York: Arno Press, 1978. 231pp. This bibliography is in two major sections: one on the black family, the other on the black woman. Each of these is subdivided by topic. There are two opening sections on periodicals and reference sources. Based on the holdings of the Indiana University Library, this is an excellent source. (Original edition: Klotman, Phyllis R. and Wilmer H. Baatz. *The Black Family and the Black Woman: A Bibliography.* Bloomington: Indiana University Library, 1972.)

227 Medicine, Beatrice. "The Role of Women in Native American Societies, A Bibliography." *Indian Historian* 8:50–54, August 1975.

228 Portillo, Cristina, Graciela Rios, and Martha Rodriguez. *Bibliography of Writings on La Mujer.* Berkeley: University of California, Chicano Studies Library, 1976. 56pp. The 264 sources listed in this pamphlet are all housed in the Chicano Studies Library at Berkeley. The citations are listed alphabetically and numbered; an index provides subject access. A second section lists periodicals. The bibliography is illustrated with a number of excellent photographs.

229 Scott, Patricia Bell. "A Critical Overview of Sex Roles Research on Black Families." *Women Studies Abstracts* 5(2):1–9, Summer 1976.

230 Terborg-Penn, R. M. "Historical Treatment of Afro-Americans in the Women's Movement, 1900–1920: A Bibliographic Essay." *Current Bibliography of African Affairs* 7:245–259, Summer 1974.

231 Williams, Ora. *American Black Women in the Arts and Social Sciences: A Bibliographic Study.* Metuchen: Scarecrow Press, 1973. 141pp. More than 1,200 works by American black women, including print and nonprint media, are listed in this bibliography. The comprehensive listing is subdivided by subject; in addition, there are sections on selected individual bibliography, a section on "Other Arts" for black women in the graphic arts and music, audio-visual aids and periodicals, and black publishing houses. There is a name index and there are selected portraits throughout.

232 ———. "A Bibliography of Works Written by American Black Women." *College Language Association Journal* 15:354–377, March 1972.

233 Willingham, Louise N. "The Black Woman: An Annotated Bibliography." *The Unabashed Librarian* 14:16–17, Winter 1975.

234 Zuckoff, Aviva Cantor. *Sixth Edition of the Annotated Bibliography on the Jewish Woman.* Fresh Meadows: Biblio Press, 1978. The new edition of this bibliography came available as we were going to press. We were able to include the new title and pub-

lishing information, but were not able to correct the change in the author's name from Aviva Cantor Zuckoff to Aviva Cantor. Thus, both Zuckoff and Cantor appear in the Author Index. Citations in this bibliography are arranged by format (books, articles, papers, fiction) and subject (Israel, history/sociology, holocaust and resistance, Jewish religion and law, America). In the post-1972 section, there is a subject division for the Jewish women's movement. (Original edition: Zuckoff, Aviva Cantor. *Bibliography on the Jewish Woman.* New York: Jewish Feminist Organization, 1975. 15 pp.)

Philosophy

Perhaps a better title for this section would be, "Written by a Professional Philosopher," since nearly every issue raised by the women's movement is a philosophical issue, and nearly every other section includes bibliographies with some philosophical writings. It is, of course, the one place to find compilations of philosophical works only.

235 Bazin, Nancy Topping. "The Concept of Androgyny: A Working Bibliography." *Women's Studies* 2(2):217–235, 1974.

236 English, Jane. "Review Essay: Philosophy." *Signs* 3(4):823–831, Summer 1978.

237 Moulton, Janice. *Philosophy and Feminism: Recent Papers.* Cambridge, 1976. 12pp. Moulton's bibliography includes journal articles (the bulk of the compilation) and unpublished papers in the following areas: Abortion, Preferential Hiring and Equal Opportunity, Language, The Nature of Women, Relations between the Sexes, Women in the History of Philosophy, The Women's Movement, and Related to Philosophical Feminism. All but one of the dated entries was published after 1970. The bibliography includes approximately 160 citations.

238 ———. "Review Essay: Philosophy." *Signs* 2(2):422–433, Winter 1976.

239 Pierce, Christine. "Review Essay: Philosophy." *Signs* 1(2):487–504, Winter 1975.

Politics

The eleven bibliographies in this section cover an array of topics: women's voting patterns and influence, women in appointive and elective office, women's role in party politics, women in goverment employment, and women's volunteer political activity. Stanwick and Li's The Political Participation of Women is the most comprehensive of the sources listed.

240 Boals, Kay. "Review Essay: Political Science." *Signs* 1(1):161–174, Autumn 1975.

241 Center for the American Woman and Politics. *Voluntary Participation among Women in the United States: A Selected Bibliography, 1950-1976.* New Brunswick, 1976. 35pp. The Center's bibliography "provides access to information about the nature, extent, and political impact of U.S. women's volunteer activities and affiliations." The material is organized into sections by form, including dissertations, unpublished works, and research in progress. "How-to" literature on recruiting, training, and keeping volunteers has not been included. There is an author index.

242 Fitch, Nancy E. *Women in Politics: The United States and Abroad, A Select Bibliography.* Washington: U.S. Library of Congress, Congressional Research Service, Governments Division, 1976. Fitch's bibliography is divided into two large sections: General Works and Biographical Works. Each of these is subdivided into American, Black American, and Foreign, as well as by format. There are approximately 150 annotated citations, about one-third of them newspaper articles.

243 Jacquette, Jane S. "Review Essay: Political Science." *Signs* 2(1):147–164, Autumn 1976.

244 Krauss, Wilma Rule. "Political Implications of Gender Roles: A Review of the Literature." *American Political Science Review* 68(4):1706–1723, December 1974. "The purpose of this essay is to introduce the reader to the contemporary literature on gender

roles and feminine behavior including the major concepts, empirical findings, and social thought which have implications for political behavior and research.'' The review has three main parts: The Contemporary Situation, Gender Roles and Women's Political Movements in Historical Perspective, and Origins of Gender Roles. More than two hundred research studies are discussed.

245 Levenson, Rosaline. *Women in Government and Politics: A Bibliography of American and Foreign Sources.* Monticello: Council of Planning Librarians, 1973. 80pp. Levenson's bibliography comes out of an interest in the long history of women's participation—or attempted participation—in government and politics since the nineteenth century. She presents more than one thousand citations, primarily to works published since 1940, but including major books and articles predating that. The bibliography is divided into four major sections: Bibliographies and Indexes; Women in Government (including the armed forces, foreign service, and judicial work); Women in Politics (including the suffrage movement and the woman voter); and Women in Government and Politics in Other Countries.

246 Levitt, Morris. *Women's Role in American Politics.* Monticello: Council of Planning Librarians, 1973. 25pp. Morris Levitt has studied the political attitudes and behavior of American women, with particular regard for the effect of education and employment on their level of participation. In a brief introduction, he discusses the results of a 1965 to 1968 survey of voters, extrapolating and analyzing the data on women. Based on this essay, it becomes clear that by ''political participation'' he means voting behavior primarily—not women in appointive or elective office. The bibliography includes scholarly books and articles, mostly from the late 1950s to early 1970s; a few earlier works are cited. Levitt has included works on voting behavior generally and on the status of women, in addition to those on women's political activities.

247 Sapiro, Virginia. *A Guide to Published Works on Women and Politics II.* 2d ed. Ann Arbor: University of Michigan, Institute for Social Research, Center for Political Studies, 1975. 81pp. The

title of Sapiro's bibliography is something of a misnomer, since her work includes a wealth of material on women's status and history, on sex roles and the women's movement, as well as on women and politics. The broad areas covered are: The Political Realm; Cross-National Studies; Sociological, Psychological, and Economic Perspectives; The Women's Movement; Black Women and Feminism; and Historical Studies. Each of these areas comprises a section of the bibliography, and each is subdivided topically. A final section lists a miscellany of items, including anthologies and bibliographies. Each section and subsection begins with a brief overview pointing out the subjects and merits of various works listed. The bibliography is limited to books and articles in English. Most of the material has been published recently.

248 Stanwick, Kathy and Christine Li. *The Political Participation of Women in the United States: A Selected Bibliography, 1950–1976.* Metuchen: Scarecrow Press, 1977. 160pp. This bibliography was prepared at the Center for the American Woman and Politics (CAWP), Rutgers University (of which Stanwick and Li are staff) and supersedes the CAWP publication, *Women and American Politics,* published in 1974. It extends the coverage of that compilation backward to 1950 (from 1965) and forward to 1976 (from 1974). The type of material cited remains the same; it includes much that is unpublished and hard to find, as well as research in progress. The subject scope is broad, including women in appointive or elective office, women's role in party politics, voting behavior, political socialization, women's lobbying and volunteer political activity, women's participation in social movements, and histories of women's political activity. The more than 1,500 citations are arranged by format: bibliographies, directories, periodicals, books, etc. A biographical index will help the researcher trace the lives of individual women; the lack of a subject index will cause the general user some problem. Finally, many of the works listed are housed at the CAWP collection, and inquiries are invited. (Original edition: Chrisman, Sara B. *Woman and American Politics: A Selected Bibliography, 1965–1974.* New Brunswick: Rutgers University, Center for the American Woman and Politics, 1974. 56pp.)

249 Swanick, M. Lynne Struthers. *Women in Canadian Politics and Government: A Bibliography*. Monticello: Council of Planning Librarians, 1974. 29pp. The purpose of this bibliography is to "bring together references to articles, books, and documents which discuss and illuminate the role and rights of women in politics and government in Canada," including the campaign for woman suffrage. The bibliography includes 245 citations arranged alphabetically and followed by a subject index. In addition, there are listings of women's magazines and newspapers, and of government bodies concerned with the status of Canadian women. This is one of the better Canadian sources since it includes Canadian material almost exclusively.

250 Whaley, Sara. "American Women in National Political Life." *Women Studies Abstracts* 1:1–9, Spring 1972. A bibliographical essay listing and discussing books and articles that contain information on the socialization of women and girls as well as the role of women in the national government, political parties, and pressure groups.

Professions

These bibliographies on women in various professions were pulled out of the Work section because they were numerous enough (there are twenty-two of them) to stand on their own. Several of them are not concerned with women in specific professions, but rather the more general "management" or "executive" category. The professions represented include librarianship, medicine, police work, architecture, geography, journalism, engineering, the sciences—a varied and interesting cross-section. As explained in the introduction, this section also includes one bibliography on prostitution.

SEE ALSO: **Work.**

251 Brugh, Anne E. and Benjamin R. Beede. "Review Essay: American Librarianship." *Signs* 1(4):943–956, Summer 1976.

252 Bullough, Vern et al. *A Bibliography of Prostitution.* New York: Garland, 1977. 419pp. Bullough's aim in compiling this bibliography was to be all-encompassing. Thus, because of the various definitions of prostitution (many of which are described in the introduction), works on "almost any aspect of extramarital sexual activity" are cited. Evidently, the subject has been a popular one—the volume includes just under 6,500 citations. Organization is either by form (including area studies, biography, and fiction) or subject (including history, legal and police regulations, sociology, and war). There are twenty chapters in all, Medicine and Public Health being the largest. The bibliography was compiled with the aid of a computer, which accounts for the unpleasant style of type. Typesetting would have made a more attractive, easier to read book, but the efficiency of the computer undoubtedly outweighed those considerations.

253 Business and Professional Women's Foundation. *Women Executives: A Selected Annotated Bibliography.* Washington, 1970. 26pp. This bibliography covers periodical articles for the most part, but also includes books, pamphlets, reports and theses. The materials themselves range from the popular and general to the scholarly; they have been published within the past ten to fifteen

years on the whole, though a few earlier pieces are included. The citations are divided into chapters by type of material. The annotations are not evaluative, and all the materials listed are available in the Foundation library.

254 ———. *Women in Positions at Managerial, Administrative and Executive Levels.* Washington, 1966. 19pp. Out of print.

255 Chaff, Sandra L. et al. *Women in Medicine: A Bibliography of the Literature on Women Physicians.* Metuchen: Scarecrow Press, 1977. 1,124pp. *Women in Medicine* is undoubtedly the major reference work on women in the medical profession. Based heavily on the Women in Medicine Collection at the Medical College of Pennsylvania (formerly the Women's Medical College), it includes more than four thousand annotated entries. The bibliography is arranged into fourteen subject chapters (history, biography, recruitment, missionary activity, wartime activity, etc.), each of which is subdivided by geography. Materials included range from the eighteenth century (the earliest dated entry is a 1750 German pamphlet) through 1975, and more than ninety percent are in English. The titles of foreign language works have been translated into English. Appendixes list directories of women physicians and special collections on women in medicine. There are author, subject, and personal name indexes totalling more than one hundred pages. Certainly, any researches into the history and status of women in medicine will have to begin here.

256 Cheda, Sherrill. "Women and Management: A Selective Bibliography 1970–1973." *Canadian Library Journal* 31(1):18–27, January/February 1974.

257 Coxe, Betsy and Florence Klemna. *Women in the Military.* Colorado Springs: U.S. Air Force Academy, Library, 1975.

258 Davis, Audrey B. *Bibliography on Women: With Special Emphasis on their Roles in Science and Society.* New York: Science History Publications, 1974. 50pp. This bibliography

covers books and articles on women in science internationally, as well as their participation in society more generally. The citations are alphabetical by author; there is no subject classification.

259   Davis, Lenwood G. *The Policewoman in American Society: A Preliminary Survey.* Monticello: Council of Planning Librarians, 1976. 15pp. Davis's bibliography is arranged by form into five sections: articles, books, pamphlets, government documents, theses and dissertations. There is no introduction to explain the bibliography's scope or purpose, but a quick survey indicates the inclusion of twentieth-century materials in English. The earliest item listed is a book dated 1909, and in the articles section especially, there are a great many works from the early part of the century through the twenties.

260   Fitzpatrick, M. Louise. "Review Essay: Nursing." *Signs* 2(4): 818–834, Summer 1977.

261   Goerss, Katherine Van Wessem. *Women Administrators in Education: A Review of Research 1960-1976.* Washington: National Association for Women Deans, Administrators and Counselors, 1977. 24pp. Goerss's review discusses more than forty research studies on the woman administrator, most of them conducted since 1970. Her paper "summarizes and compares the personal, educational, professional, and psychological characteristics of women administrators who hold low-level and upper-echelon positions in public schools, public and private colleges and universities and professional organizations in all areas of the United States."

262   Haist, Dianne. *Women in Management: A Selected Bibliography, 1970-1975.* Toronto: Ontario Ministry of Labour, Research Library, 1976. 18pp. The bibliography is divided into four sections: monographs, articles, periodicals, and bibliographies. The Canadian items—the minority—are starred.

263   Hayden, Dolores and Gwendolyn Wright. "Review Essay: Architecture and Urban Planning." *Signs* 1(4):923–934, Summer 1976.

264   Healy, Barbara R. *Women in Management: A Selected Anno-tated Bibliography of Current and Cited Books and Articles*. Rochester: University of Rochester, Management Library, 1974.

265   Heim, Kathleen and Kathleen Weibel. *The Role of Women in Librarianship 1876–1976: The Entry, Advancement and Struggle for Equalization in One Profession*. New York: Neal-Schuman Publishers, forthcoming. In the past, the American Library Association has distributed a bibliography on women in librarianship compiled and updated by different members of its Task Force on Women. That will probably no longer be the case (or at least not for the current compilation), because a greatly expanded version of that bibliography will appear in Heim and Weibel's anthology, *The Role of Women in Librarianship*. This entry is the one exception to the "separately-published bibliography rule" which guides the compilation of this volume. I have made an exception in this case for two reasons: the nearness of the topic to my librarian's heart and the size and scope of the bibliography. *The Role of Women in Librarianship* is not in print as of this writing; however, the bibliography section has been completed and is three hundred manuscript pages. It would appear that the bibliography will dwarf the anthology and not vice versa.

266   Jacquet, C. H. "Professional Woman in the United States: A Bibliographical Essay." *Information Service* 48:1–7, May 1969.

267   Johnson, Carolyn R. *Women in Architecture: An Annotated Bibliography and Guide to Sources of Information*. Monticello: Council of Planning Librarians, 1974. 25pp. Johnson has brought together writings (books and periodical articles) on opportunities for women in architecture, on the achievements of women architects, studies and surveys of women architects, and women in related career fields. Each one of the broad areas forms a section of the bibliography, which then lists works in chronological order. There is a listing of organizations and associations of women architects and a listing of statistical sources. Each item is carefully annotated.

268   Loyd, Bonnie. *Women and Geography: An Annotated Bibliography and Guide to Sources of Information*. Monticello: Council

of Planning Librarians, 1976. 18pp. Loyd's bibliography lists materials of two types: works on the woman geographer, her status and participation; and geographical studies on women. The pamphlet is divided into these two sections, both of which contain a miscellany of materials—films, conferences, articles, organizations, and research in progress. Everything listed is very recent, most of it from 1970.

269   Marzolf, Marion, Ramona R. Rush, and Darlene Stern. "The Literature of Women in Journalism History." *Journalism History* 1(4):117–128, Winter 1974/75.

270   Roysdon, Christy. *Women in Engineering: A Bibliography on their Progress and Prospects.* Monticello: Council of Planning Librarians, 1975. 22pp. Roysdon has divided her bibliography into eight major subject areas which provide a good description of the literature cited. The sections are Background: The Professional Woman; Major Books (those dealing specifically with the woman engineer); The Status of Women Engineers: Numbers, Trends; Recruitment: The Chronic Problem; Education and Training; On the Job: Performance, Opportunity, Satisfaction; Role Models—Success Stories; and Government Documents. There are two nonbibliographic sections listing major conferences and relevant organizations. Items of particular interest and those with vague titles have been annotated briefly.

271   Vetter, Betty M. "Review Essay: Women in the Natural Sciences." *Signs* 1(3):713–720, Spring 1976.

272   Williams, Martha, Jean Oliver, and Meg Gerrard. *Women in Management: A Selected Bibliography.* Austin: University of Texas, School of Social Work, Center for Social Work Research, 1977. 64pp. Work on this bibliography began in 1975 in preparation for a conference, "Women in Management," sponsored by the University of Texas that spring. Collection of these materials continued in an effort to develop a special library on the managerial woman. The bibliography includes selected books, journal articles, and unpublished papers of recent vintage. The more

than six hundred citations fall into seven issue areas with a chapter for each: women in the work force generally, the legal issues, internal (psychological) factors, personal/work roles and conflicts, women as leaders, organizational barriers to women's participation, and strategies for change. Each of these chapters has a brief introduction describing the major issues and setting them in historical context. The best source I have found in the area.

Psychology

The psychology section is substantial, with a number of excellent sources. However, there is nothing comprehensive that is recent. Sherman's book-length review essay was published in 1971, Walstedt's The Psychology of Women in 1972, and the American Psychological Association's A Topical Bibliography in 1974. The most recent entry is Vaughter's review essay in the Autumn 1976 issue of Signs. While this is an excellent source for current research, it is not comprehensive. The Signs review essays will continue to be an important resource in this area.

SEE ALSO: Sex Roles and Sex Differences.

273 Baer, Helen R. and Carolyn W. Sherif. *A Topical Bibliography (Selectively Annotated) on Psychology of Women*. Washington: American Psychological Association, 1974. 104pp. More than one thousand works are cited in this selected bibliography on the psychology of women. It covers a broad range of topics, from history to feminism to anthropology, and is not, strictly speaking, concerned only with female psychology. Certain major books and articles have been annotated; some of the books chapter by chapter. The section titles are: Historical Perspectives; Contemporary Women's Movement; Biological Basis for Sex Differences; Critique of Research and Theory on Sex Differences; Cross-Cultural Perspectives; Psychological Development; Research on Cognitive Differences and Achievement; Sexuality and Reproduction; Psychological Problems of Women; and Aging.

274 Carey, Emily A. *Issues in the Psychology and Counseling of Women*. Boston: Womanspace: Feminist Therapy Collective, 1976. 19pp. Approximately half of this mimeographed bibliography is a straight alphabetical listing of citations. Then follow two brief subject sections: Women and Alcoholism, Lesbians and Mental Health.

275 ——, Bianca Murphy, and Charlotte Wasserman. *Counseling Women: A Bibliography*. Boston: Womanspace: Feminist Therapy Collective, 1975. 12pp. *Counseling Women* is a straight alphabetical listing of citations; there are no annotations.

276 Cromwell, Phyllis E. *Women and Mental Health, Selected Annotated References 1970-1973.* Rockville: National Institute of Mental Health, Division of Scientific and Technical Information, 1974. 247pp. Out of print.

277 Henley, Nancy. "Resources for the Study of Psychology and Women." *RT: Journal of Radical Therapy* 4:20–21, December 1974.

278 Javonovich, Joann et al. *Women and Psychology.* Cambridge: Cambridge-Goddard Graduate School for Social Change, 1972. 36pp. Out of print. This selected, annotated bibliography is an outgrowth of the Psychology and Woman Seminar of the Feminist Studies Program at the Cambridge-Goddard Graduate School. Originally compiled in 1972, it was reprinted, but not revised, by the New England Free Press. Each section of the bibliography is preceded by an introduction describing how and why the particular materials were selected. The compilers approach the material with a feminist point of view. The sections include: Philosophy of Science, Methodology and Statistical Uses, History of Psychology, Sex Differences, Sex Role Development and Socialization of Children, Individual Psychology and Personality Theory, Individual Development and Group Dynamics, The Small Group in the Development of Political Organization. Citations are listed alphabetically by author.

279 Parlee, Mary Brown. "Review Essay: Psychology." *Signs* 1(1): 119–138, Autumn 1975.

280 Sherman, Julia Ann. *On the Psychology of Women: A Survey of Empirical Studies.* Springfield: Charles C. Thomas, 1971. 304pp. This literature review examines more than nine hundred works of research in the psychology of women. The research falls into eleven major areas (there is a chapter on each): Biology of Sex Differences, Psychology of Sex Differences, Freudian Theory of Feminine Development, Female Oedipus Complex, Moral and Sex Role Development, Adolescence, Cyclic Changes, Female Sexuality, Pregnancy, Motherhood, and The Later Years.

281   Vaughter, Reesa M. "Review Essay: Psychology." *Signs* 2(1): 120–146, Autumn 1976.

282   Walstedt, Joyce Jennings. *The Psychology of Women: A Partially Annotated Bibliography.* Pittsburgh: KNOW, 1972. 76pp. Part I of this bibliography is arranged according to the stages in women's lives: Infancy and Childhood, Adolescence, Young Adulthood, Middle and Old Age. Part II has six thematic subcategories: Cross Cultural; General Source Material; Primate Studies; Minority Group Status, Discrimination; Psychoanalytic Theories, Mental Health; and Sexuality and Physiology. It should be clear from this list of categories that the bibliography covers a wide range of materials, though the majority of the citations are to research articles in academic journals. The bibliography is not meant to be exhaustive, except in the case of journal articles published since 1970. Walstedt searched all the major psychological journals from 1970 for relevant entries and annotated all of them. All post-1970 materials are marked with an asterisk, and those considered to be of special interest are also marked. The annotations are "neutral" and descriptive. In cases where Walstedt had a strong opinion, she has given it in a separate paragraph labelled "Comments." Both the annotations and the comments are incisive and very helpful. The only drawback to this bibliography is its age.

Rape

Rape has been a crucial topic in feminist literature since the publication of Susan Griffin's "Rape: The All-American Crime" (Ramparts, Vol. 10, No. 3) in 1971. More recently, it has been taken seriously as a research area by criminologists and psychologists, and several bibliographies of scholarly writing have appeared.

283 Albin, Rochelle Semmel. "Review Essay: Psychological Studies of Rape." *Signs* 3(2):423–435, Winter 1977.

284 Barnes, Dorothy L. *Rape: A Bibliography, 1965–1975.* Troy: Whitson Publishing, 1977.

285 Chappell, Duncan, Gilbert Geis, and Faith Fogarty. "Forcible Rape: Bibliography." *The Journal of Criminal Law and Criminology* 65(2):248–263, 1974. This bibliography is organized by subject with careful cross-referencing of the more than three hundred items. The introduction points out the shift in the tone of the material pre- and post-women's movement. The subject categories include Sociology, Victim, Offender, Law, Medical and Police Investigation. There is an author index.

286 Kemmer, Elizabeth Jane. *Rape and Rape-Related Issues: An Annotated Bibliography.* New York: Garland, 1977, 174pp. This slim volume contains 348 citations to rape literature in English from 1965 to 1976. The annotations are detailed and helpful. There is a list of the 150 periodicals cited and a good subject index; the citations themselves are not arranged by subject, but listed alphabetically by main entry. However, it is always upsetting to see the publisher skimp on the production (the body of the book is typed, not typeset) of such a worthwhile book.

287 St. Louis Feminist Research Project. *The Rape Bibliography: A Collection of Abstracts.* St. Louis, 1977. 93pp. *The Rape Bibliography* covers scholarly writing on four aspects of rape: legal, medical, psychological, and sociological. Each of these sections is divided into "Bibliography," which cites works written before

1970, and "Abstracts," which cites and annotates works written after 1970. A final section, "Popular Press," covers all nonscholarly work on the four aspects published after 1970. The recent acceptance of rape as a legitimate and crucial problem for our society is evidenced by the ratio of post- to pre-1970 works. Out of a total 443 citations, 169—or about forty percent—are in the post-1970 period. This bibliography is an excellent resource for researchers tackling this disturbing issue.

288   Schwendinger, Julia R. and Herman Schwendinger. "A Review of Rape Literature." *Crime and Social Justice* 6:79–85, Fall/Winter 1976.

Reference Sources

This is one of the sections which did not exist in the original compilation, but has developed rapidly since 1974. The concept of reference service on women's issues has followed in the footsteps of women's studies research; it is now of concern to many librarians. In fact, most of these bibliographies were compiled by college and university librarians who developed their specialty in response to their campus's women's studies program.

289 Eichler, Margrit and Sara Whaley. "A Bibliography of Canadian and United States, Resources on Women." *Women Studies Abstracts* 2(4):1, Fall 1973 and 3(1):1, Winter 1974. Eichler and Whaley list and discuss reference works and bibliographies on women in Canada and the United States, including those published over the preceding ten years as well as a few that are still forthcoming. Their essay is arranged into sections by form: reference books, bibliographies, and other library resources (mostly indexes and abstracts), with a final section on the as yet unpublished works.

290 Hoffman, Ruth H. *Women: A Basic Guide to Research.* Bowling Green: Bowling Green State University Libraries, 1978. 25pp. Hoffman's research guide is typical of its type, giving a basic introduction to the card catalog, appropriate subject headings, general and specialized reference sources. It includes as well, a list of local women's programs and services.

291 Lynn, Naomi B., Ann B. Matasar, and Marie Barovic Rosenberg. *Research Guide in Women's Studies.* Morristown: General Learning Press, 1974. 194pp. This is a college-level introduction to social science research, reference work, and writing of women's studies research papers. Many college or university libraries have put out similar guides for their own students.

292 Mateer, Carolyn, Rae Rohfeld, and Laverne Zell. *Research Guide to Women's Issues.* Cleveland: Cleveland State University, Institute of Urban Affairs, Clearinghouse for Research on Women and Employment, 1976. 37pp. Out of print. *Research Guide to Women's Issues* is much like the other guides in this

section. In addition to describing basic research procedures and reference sources, it also provides a series of suggestions for research needed in three major areas: education, conditions of employment, and implementation of equal employment opportunities. The final section is a reprint of "Research and Support Strategies for Women's Higher Education," a paper prepared by the Project on the Status and Education of Women.

293 McKee, Kathleen Burke. *Women's Studies: A Guide to Reference Sources.* Storrs: The University of Connecticut Library, 1977. 112pp. This attractive paperback includes 364 citations to specialized and general reference sources in the University of Connecticut Library. Arranged by type of publication, the compilation covers guides; library catalogs; handbooks; directories; statistical sources; indexes, abstracts, and bibliographies. Subdivisions by form and/or subject are provided where necessary; the indexes, abstracts, and bibliographies section, for example, is broken down into more than twenty subject areas. A final section, compiled by Joanne V. Akeroyd, lists feminist serials found in the library's Alternative Press Collection. The holdings as of January 1977 are given for each title, along with a description of the type of periodical and its usual contents. There are subject, author, and title indexes. This is an excellent guide to reference sources in women's studies and should be useful to a wide audience beyond the University of Connecticut.

294 Papazian, Barbara and Ernestine Snead. *Finding Materials by and about Women in the Michigan State University Libraries.* East Lansing: Michigan State University Libraries, 1977. 21pp. The M.S.U. Libraries have a "How to Find" series, of which this manual is a part. While it is basically a guide to library research, it lists a variety of reference sources. The sections are delineated by the type of information sought: Finding Books, Finding Newspaper and Periodical Articles, Finding Biographical Information, etc.

295 Schlachter, Gail and Donna Belli. *The Changing Role of Women in America: A Selected Annotated Bibliography of Reference Sources.* Monticello: Council of Planning Librarians, 1975. 36pp. Schlachter and Belli have divided their guide to reference

works into two parts: Information Sources, which includes directories, encyclopedias, biographical dictionaries, and so forth; and Citation Sources, which actually means bibliographies. This compilation is less extensive than the McKee guide (#293); it lists only sources which are devoted exclusively to women and not the more general ones which may have sections on women. Foreign language materials and minor or obscure items are not included. Each entry is carefully annotated; the annotations are descriptive rather than evaluative. There are author and title indexes. In general, a good source.

296 ———. *Minorities and Women: A Guide to Reference Literature in the Social Sciences.* Los Angeles: Reference Service Press, 1977. 349pp. Schlachter and Belli's *Guide* is somewhat outside the scope of this compilation in that it is not devoted exclusively to works on women. I have included it, nevertheless, for two reasons: one, it contains substantial material on women (approximately 130 citations) and two, because the sources on minority women are few, the works on minorities in general might provide a useful lead. The volume is divided into two parts: Information Sources, subdivided by form (fact books, biographical sources, document sources, directories, statistical sources); and Citation Sources, subdivided by type of person (Minorities, American Indians, Asian Americans, Black Americans, Spanish Americans, Women). Materials were considered for inclusion if written in English, recently published (or classics), commercially available, and on at least a high school level. Every item is annotated, and there are author, title, and subject indexes. The resemblance between this work and their *The Changing Role of Women* will be noted.

297 Seckelson-Simpson, Linda. *With Reference to Women: An Annotated Bibliography of Reference Materials on Women in the Northwestern University Library.* Evanston: Northwestern University Library, 1975. 55pp. *With Reference to Women* lists general and specialized reference sources in five subject areas. The 157 entries are carefully annotated in some detail. In addition to the straight bibliography sections, there are lists of women's organizations and special library collections on women. An excellent resource.

298 Woodsworth, Anne and Jane Clark. *Women: A Guide to Bibliographic Sources.* 2d ed. Toronto: University of Toronto, John P. Robarts Research Library, 1974. 26pp. This bibliography of reference sources was compiled by Anne Woodsworth; it first appeared in 1972, with an addenda in 1973. The revision was done by Jane Clark and essentially combines the first edition and its addenda into one. The only revision is the interfiling of the two parts, there are no substantial additions (a total increase of three citations), nor have the basic outline or annotations changed. The *Guide* has five major sections: The Card Catalogues, Sources in the Reference Room, The Government Publications Section, Women's Periodicals, and Sources Outside the University. The bulk of the compilation (fifteen out of twenty-six pages) is the reference room section, which is broken down into subcategories for bibliographies, biographical dictionaries, course syllabi, directories and encyclopedias, and indexes and abstracts. The annotations are brief but informative. There is an author/title index. Although this *Guide* is now a bit dated, it is still useful, especially for Canadian sources. (Original edition: Woodsworth, Anne. *Women: A Guide to Bibliographic Sources in the University of Toronto Library.* Toronto: University of Toronto, Library, 1972. 7pp. *Addenda.* 1973. 14pp.)

299 Wright, Maureen. *Women's Studies: A Student's Guide to Reference Sources.* ERIC, 1975, 12pp. (ED 117 747). Wright divides her bibliography into four main sections: Directories, Encyclopedias, Biographical Sources, and Bibliographies. The bibliography section is subdivided by topic and comprises half of the publication. Each entry is carefully annotated. This is a good all-around source, but is especially useful for reference material on Canadian women.

Religion

The bibliographies in this section represent the variety of contemporary issues concerning women and religion: the status of women in the church, feminist interpretations of theology, the ordination of women.

300 Bass, Dorothy. *American Women in Church and Society, 1607-1920: A Bibliography*. New York: Auburn Theological Seminary, 1973. 37pp. The title of this bibliography is perhaps a bit misleading as it includes material on women in a wide variety of topics in addition to women and the church. There is, however, one lengthy section devoted to the church as well as one on sects and utopias. There are numerous works in other sections that are written by ministers or that concern the way Christianity has affected women. The partially-annotated citations are arranged into chapters broadly by subject, they then are further subdivided.

301 Cerling, C.E. "An Annotated Bibliography of the New Testament Teachings about Women." *Journal of the Evangelical Theology Society* 16(1):47-53, 1973.

302 Christ, Carol P. "Feminist Studies in Religion and Literature: A Methodological Reflection." *Journal of the American Academy of Religion* 44:317-326, June 1976.

303 Driver, Anne Barstow. "Review Essay: Religion." *Signs* 2(2): 434-442, Winter 1976.

304 Farians, Elizabeth. *Women and Religion: Selected Bibliography, 1965-1972*. Cincinnati, 1973. 29pp. Farians's self-published bibliography is arranged first by form of material (books, articles, bibliographies, films, packets, reports, newsletters, special periodical issues) and then chronologically. The largest section by far is the compilation of articles. There is also a brief listing of women's religious and church organizations.

305 Fischer, Clare B. and Rochelle Gatlin. *Woman: A Theological Perspective: Bibliography and Addendum*. Berkeley: Graduate

Theological Union, Office of Women's Affairs, 1975. 47pp. Like Dorothy Bass's compilation (#300), *Woman: A Theological Perspective* includes a broad spectrum of material which ranges beyond works specifically on women and religious concerns. Fischer and Gatlin explain in their introduction that they have assumed an "elastic interpretation of what theological inquiry is about." They do not, however, specifically explain *how* the additional works have been selected beyond noting the interdisciplinary nature of women's studies, and need to understand the general history and status of women, and the parameters of feminist thinking. The bibliography is divided into nine sections: Bibliography and Resources; Women and—Scripture, History, Theology, Society, Psychology, Socialization, Art; and Women in Comparative Perspective. These are further subdivided, sometimes by form (books, articles), sometimes by subject. The compilation is eclectic and interesting, undoubtedly reflecting the concerns and interests of the editors. It is also quite substantial, approaching one thousand citations.

306 Kendall, Patricia A. *Women and the Priesthood: A Selected and Annotated Bibliography*. Philadelphia: Episcopal Diocese of Pennsylvania, 1976. 57pp. This bibliography was prepared as part of the work of the Committee to Promote the Cause of and to Plan for the Ordination of Women, appointed by the Diocese in 1974. Since the Committee's approach to the problem of the ordination of women was one of advocacy, so are the works cited in the bibliography. The primary objective was to compile materials providing "sound theological reasons for the ordination of women." The bibliography was designed for a lay audience, thus some interesting but difficult sources were not cited. The annotations are substantial; in the case of anthologies, each individual article is annotated.

307 Kirby, Kathryn E. *Status of Women in the Church: Vatican II, 1968; Annotated Bibliography*. Washington: Catholic University of America. Department of Library Science, 1970. 52pp. Out of print. Although this bibliography is out of print, the Library School Library has one copy that they will xerox at cost; from: Library, Department of Library Science, Catholic University, Washington, DC 20064.

308 Patrick, Anne E. "Women and Religion: A Survey of Significant Literature, 1965–1974." *Theological Studies* 36:737–765, December 1975.

309 Porter, Harry B. "Women Priests: Some Recent Literature." *Anglican Theological Review* 2:83–87, 1973.

310 Way, Peggy A. "Women, the Church and Liberation: A Growth Oriented Bibliography." *Dialog* 10:93–103, Spring 1971.

311 Wilson, Martha M. "Women and the Church." *Duke Divinity School Review* 38:100–102, Spring 1973.

Sex Roles and Sex Differences

The degree to which the differences exhibited by men and women are due to nature—or to learned, sex-typed behavior—is now the object of much study. This section includes a number of bibliographies on sex-role research in general, the most comprehensive of which is Astin's Sex Roles: A Research Bibliography. Other bibliographies provide access to the literature on sex-stereotyped images in the media, sex differences in language, and sex differences in reading achievement.

SEE ALSO: Sociology; Psychology.

312 Astin, Helen et al. *Sex Roles: A Research Bibliography.* Washington: National Institute of Mental Health, 1975. 362pp. This compilation is a substantial one (450 entries); probably the major bibliography of sex-role research. An initial search of the literature was made to determine a general framework of the research and to facilitate development of categories. Then, the categories were "filled in" with selections, giving an overview of the entire field. That is, the different areas of research were "highlighted" by an entry or two instead of being covered exhaustively. The studies cited range from 1960 to 1972, and the emphasis is on literature with an empirical basis. Thus, only a few feminist works are included. The bibliography is divided into five categories: sex differences; the origin of sex differences and development of sex roles; the manifestation of sex roles in various settings (family, work, school); overviews of the status of the sexes; and general reviews and theory on the process of socialization. Because these categories are broad and the research is often very specific and technical, a detailed subject index is included and should be used. The annotations are substantial and descriptive, generally running to two or three paragraphs. In addition to the subject index, subject descriptors printed in bold face are included with each citation. Overall, an indispensable volume.

313 Friedman, Leslie J. *Sex Role Stereotyping in the Mass Media: An Annotated Bibliography.* New York: Garland, 1977. 324pp. Friedman's bibliography covers all aspects of the communications media and is divided into sections by form:

mass media, advertising, broadcast, film, print, and popular culture (comics, science fiction, pornography). There are also sections on the media image of minority women and of men, on children's media, and on the impact of all this media on occupational choice. Works cited cover a broad range, from scholarly research studies to content analysis to feminist tracts to opinion polls. The annotations are incisive and very helpful. The introduction gives a good, brief overview of the problems of media stereotyping. There are author and subject indexes. An excellent reference tool for anyone doing research in the field.

314 Henley, Nancy and Barrie Thorne. *She Said/He Said: An Annotated Bibliography of Sex Differences in Language, Speech, and Nonverbal Communication*. Pittsburgh: KNOW, 1975. 311pp. This is a bibliography that has had a pre-publication life. Compilation began in 1972, and various informal editions circulated before this paper edition was published. It is divided into nine chapters: Comprehensive Sources; Vocabulary and Syntax; Phonology; Conversational Patterns; Women's and Men's Languages, Dialects; Multilingual Situations; Language and Acquisition; Verbal Ability; and Nonverbal Aspects of Communication. The annotations are thorough—many run to nearly a page in length. A final section lists women's organizations that are concerned with language issues. There is an author index.

315 Hochschild, Arlie Russell. "A Review of Sex Role Research." *American Journal of Sociology*. 78(4):1011–1029, January 1973.

316 Lipman-Blumen, Jean. "Changing Sex Roles in American Culture: Future Directions for Research." *Archives of Sexual Behavior* 4(4):433–446, 1975.

317 ——— and Ann R. Tickamyer. "Sex Roles in Transition: A Ten-Year Perspective." *Annual Review of Sociology* 1:297–337, 1975.

318 Maferr Foundation. *Bibliography, Male-Female Role Research*. New York, 1976. 23pp. The Maferr Foundation has sponsored research on male-female roles since 1966; many of the

publications cited in this bibliography are the result of that research. The citations are organized into seven sections according to form (papers, symposia, articles) and are listed chronologically within each section.

319 Sheridan, E. Marcia. *Sex Differences and Reading: An Annotated Bibliography.* Newark: International Reading Association, 1976. 40pp. Marcia Sheridan has reviewed the fairly substantial research on reading and reading achievement, using sex as a variable. Most of this literature has been published since the mid- to late sixties; only a dozen or so of the more than 150 titles predate 1960. Sheridan has grouped the citations according to the overall concern or topic of the research. This produces nine major sections, in addition to the general one on sex differences in reading; they are: Sex Differences Based on Reading Methods, Materials and Sex Differences, Sex of Teacher, Separate Sex Classes, Differences in Treatment of Boys and Girls, Sex Differences in Interest and Attitude, Sex Differences in Achievement, Cognitive and Psychological Sex Differences, Development of Sex Role. Each citation has an annotation that briefly summarizes the research.

320 Spiegel, Jeanne. *Sex Role Concepts: How Women and Men See Themselves and Each Other; A Selected Annotated Bibliography.* Washington: Business and Professional Women's Foundation, 1969. 31pp. This bibliography covers books, pamphlets, reports, theses, articles, and microfilm, all of which are available in the Foundation library. The citations are organized by type of material into chapters, and then listed alphabetically by author. The annotations are nonevaluative. The material included is limited to that published in the last fifteen years; it covers a wide spectrum—from the popular to the scholarly.

321 Tresemer, David. *Research on Fear of Success: Full Annotated Bibliography.* Washington: American Psychological Association, 1975. 179pp. In 1968, psychologist Matina Horner conducted a pioneering study on women's attitudes toward success out of which the "fear of success" construct was born. Since then, a great variety of research has been based on this construct. Tresemer has pulled together 186 citations to 155 studies which

followed Horner's, fully describing each one. The annotations provide information on the number and type of subjects used, details of measurement techniques employed, and full results of the study. Papers collected in the course of compiling the bibliography have been donated to the Sophia Smith Library at Smith College where they form the ''Fear of Success Collection.''

Third-World Countries

This section focuses on three Third-World areas: Africa, India, and Latin America. Although many of the bibliographies in this section were not available for review, one can assume that the concentration on these particular geographical areas stems from the same research concerns seen in the Women and Development section—the crucial role of women in national economic development.

SEE ALSO: Women and Development; Minority and Ethnic Women.

AFRICA

322 African Bibliographic Centre, Women's Africa Committee, African-American Institute. *Contemporary African Women: An Introductory Bibliographical Overview and a Guide to Women's Organizations, 1960-67.* New York: Negro University Press, 1969. Out of print.

323 Al-Qazzaz, Ayad. *Women in the Middle East and North Africa: An Annotated Bibliography.* Austin: University of Texas, Center for Middle Eastern Studies, 1977. 178pp.

324 Dryden, P.K. "Annotated Bibliography of Political Rights of African Women." *African Law Studies* 7:27–62, 1972.

325 Murray, Jocelyn. *Bibliography on African Women.* Los Angeles: University of California, African Studies Center, 1974. Out of print.

326 Westfall, Gloria D. "Nigerian Women: A Bibliographical Essay." *Africana Journal* 5:99–138, Summer 1974.

INDIA

327 Dasgupta, Kalpana. *Women on the Indian Scene: An Annotated Bibliography.* New Delhi: Abhinav Publications, 1976. 392pp.

328 Lakhanpal, Sarv K. "Indian Women." *Bulletin of Bibliography* 27:38–41, April/June 1970.

329   ———. *Indian Women: A Bibliography.* Saskatoon: University of Saskatchewan, 1967. 14pp.

330   Pearce, Margaret. "Bibliography: Women In India." *Hecate* 1:90–95, January 1975.

331   Young, Katherine K. and Arvind Sharma. *Image of the Feminine; Mythic, Philosophic and Human; in the Buddhist, Hindu and Islamic Traditions: A Bibliography of Women in India.* Chico: New Horizons Press, 1974. 36pp.

LATIN AMERICA

332   Knaster, Meri. *Women in Spanish America: An Annotated Bibliography from Pre-Conquest to Contemporary Times.* Boston: G.K. Hall, 1977. 696pp. This excellent bibliography attempts to be comprehensive and, by the size of it, appears to have succeeded. Geographically, it includes only the Spanish-speaking countries of Latin America. The earliest publications listed date from the seventeenth century, and there is nothing published after 1974. All material is in Spanish or English. There are fourteen major subject sections, with a geographical break-down under each for Spanish America generally, Middle America, South America, and the Caribbean. There is a limited listing of Ph.D. and M.A. theses in the area. Scope notes begin each section and there are subject and author indexes.

333   Valdes, Nelson, P. "A Bibliography on Cuban Women in the Twentieth Century." *Cuban Studies Newsletter* 4(2):1–31, June 1974. "A Bibliography on Cuban Women" has two major parts: one on women in the prerevolutionary period (1900–1958) and the other on the revolution and after (1959–1973). The second section is about three times the size of the first. Each of the two parts has topical subcategories covering such areas as labor and production, social structure, family life, sex, politics, etc; the same categories were used for both parts to facilitate comparison. The literature deals primarily with the "socio-political-economic aspects" of women's lives in Cuba. About one-third of the 568 entries are briefly annotated, usually not more than a sentence.

Women and Development

As the research into women's position in and contribution to society has grown, it has become cross-national in scope, and recently, women in world development has been the focus of much study. Women are now seen as a potential resource whose active participation in the labor force could tip the balance in the direction of prosperity for many developing economies. Bibliographies on population studies are listed here, because research into fertility and population is usually related to the economic status and labor force participation of women.

334 American Council of Voluntary Agencies for Foreign Services, Technical Assistance Information Clearinghouse. *Women: A Bibliography, 1975-6.* New York, 1976. 30pp. The Council frequently issues an updated bibliography of TAICH holdings on women. The materials are mostly on women and development, many of them are government and United Nations publications. Entries are briefly annotated.

335 Birdsall, Nancy. "Review Essay: Women and Population Studies." *Signs* 1(3):699–712, Spring 1976.

336 Buvinic, Myra. *Women and World Development: An Annotated Bibliography.* Washington: Overseas Development Council, 1976. 162pp. Buvinic's bibliography is a companion volume to *Women and World Development*, edited by Irene Tinker and Michele Bo Bramsen, a summary of the proceedings of a 1975 seminar on women and development sponsored by the Association for the Advancement of Science. Buvinic focuses on works concerning "the effects of socio-economic development and cultural change on women and on women's reactions to these changes." The bibliography has two stated objectives: first, to disseminate the information more widely since many of the studies listed are unpublished and second, to provide an overall view of the status of research. An introductory critical review discusses various areas of research and makes suggestions for the direction of future study. There are nine broad subject divisions,

each of which is divided geographically (multi-regional, Latin America and Caribbean, North Africa and Middle East, sub-Saharan Africa, Asia and Pacific, Europe and North America). Each citation is carefully annotated. An appendix lists other related bibliographies and special issues of periodicals on women and development. There is an author index.

337　Keiffer, Miriam. "Population Limitation and Women's Status: A Bibliography." *Annals of the New York Academy of Science* 175:1039, 1970.

338　Lear, Julia G. *The Impact of Economic Development and Social Change on the Status of Women: A Select Bibliography.* Washington: Society for International Development, Committee on Women in Development, 1973. Out of print.

339　Rihani, May. *Development As If Women Mattered: An Annotated Bibliography with a Third World Focus.* Washington: New TransCentury Foundation, Secretariat for Women in Development, 1978. 137pp. The compilation of this excellent bibliography was guided by several considerations: the need for program/action-oriented materials, the location of unpublished works, the inclusion of documents authored primarily by Third-World writers, and concentration on recent sources. The 287 annotated entries are classified by subject into ten chapters; each of these is subdivided by geographical area (multi-regional, Asia and the Pacific, Latin America and the Caribbean, Middle East and North Africa, sub-Saharan Africa). Extensive cross-referencing should provide all the additional subject access a user needs. In an introductory essay, Rihani summarizes the crucial concerns in planning for development "as if women mattered"; she also provides a survey of the findings and recommendations of the works listed in each section. This is a fine publication which should find many grateful users.

340　Sharma, Prakash C. *Female Working Role and Economic Development: A Selected Research Bibliography.* Monticello: Council of Planning Librarians, 1974. 16pp. Sharma has compiled nearly 250 citations to works on women's work and economic development published between 1940 and 1972. The bibliography is arranged by form of material into two sections: books/monographs and periodical articles.

341   United Nations, Food and Agricultural Organization. *Women and Family in Rural Development: Annotated Biliography*. New York, 1977. 56pp. This is a computer-generated index of FAO documents published between 1966 and 1976.

Women's Movement

Both the first and second wave of the women's movement are represented in this section's bibliographies. Six large volumes have been published since 1972, and one is encouraged both by the quantity and the range of feminist writing.

342 Franklin, Margaret Ladd. *The Case for Woman Suffrage: A Bibliography.* New York: National College Equal Suffrage League, 1913. 315pp. Reprint. Washington: Zenger Publishing, 1976. *The Case for Woman Suffrage* is the only bibliography I've found that comes close to being a "first wave" counterpart of the recent bibliographies in women's studies.   Like many of the bibliographies here, it came from a strong social movement and was compiled with the college student in mind. The citations are arranged first by form (books, Congressional reports, leaflets, plays, periodical articles, contemporary suffrage periodicals) and then chronologically. The books section opens with a citation to Plato's *Republic;* it then jumps to the sixteenth century, covering the period from 1532 to 1911. There are a number of citations to pre-Wollstonecraft works. The Congressional documents section covers the period from 1874 to 1912, and the articles section from 1839 to 1912. Franklin has not defined her field narrowly and covers much more than the "case for woman suffrage," including a wide range of works on the need for women's economic, legal, and social equality. Most of the entries are annotated, some at length, and for the most part in a very engaging style. Franklin is not afraid to criticize and lets you know just what she thinks. The bibliography is available in a reprint edition and is an invaluable source.

343 Grimstad, Kirsten and Susan Rennie. *The New Woman's Survival Catalog.* New York: Coward, McCann and Geoghegan, 1973. 223pp. Out of print. This "Whole Earth Catalog" of the women's movement is not, strictly speaking, a bibliography. It warrants inclusion here, however, not only for the very substantial bibliographic function it does serve, but also as a movement "classic." The organization is somewhat disorderly, the coverage and text a bit uneven, but then so is the movement it catalogs.

344 ———. *The New Woman's Survival Sourcebook.* New York: Alfred A. Knopf, 1975. 245pp. A slightly different title and new publisher do not disguise what is the sequel to the *Catalog* listed above. While this volume is better organized and more thorough, it too reflects the diverse and ever-changing nature of the women's movement.

345 Krichmar, Albert. *The Women's Movement in the Seventies: An International English-Language Bibliography.* Metuchen: Scarecrow Press, 1977. 875pp. At first glance, the most noticeable aspect of this bibliography is its sheer size: 875 pages, nearly ten thousand citations, two and one-half inches thick, and weighing nearly three pounds. Enough to make the most stalwart bibliographer's head swim. Inside, however, the volume is organized so as to be quite comprehensible and easy to use. It is arranged geographically into nine major sections: International, Africa, Asia, Australia and Oceania, Europe, Latin America, Mid East, North America—Canada, North America—United States. Each of these primary continent divisions is subdivided two ways: by subject and by geographical area (country, state, or province). The subject divisions, which are uniform throughout, are: General, Cultural and Literary, Legal and Political, Psychological, Religious and Philosophical, Scientific and Technical, Sociological and Anthropological Studies. Works listed include Ph.D. dissertations, books, pamphlets, research reports, periodical articles, and government documents published between 1970 and 1975. They are English-language publications on the status of women in society with the emphasis "on change, attempted change, and continuing problems confronting women in the countries in which they live." Approximately seventy-five percent of the volume is devoted to the section on the United States, though not by design. The next largest section by country is the United Kingdom, with only six percent of the total; the drop is fairly dramatic. A little more than five thousand of the entries are annotated, or about sixty percent overall. This percentage is not uniform, however, with a greater proportion of the U.S. materials annotated. A final major section lists just over two hundred reference works. There is a complete author index and a substantial subject index of nearly one hundred pages.

346 ———. *The Women's Rights Movement in the U.S., 1848-1970.* Metuchen: Scarecrow Press, 1972. 436pp. This is more than just a bibliography, it is a handbook for anyone beginning serious study of the history of women's rights. Bringing together much important literature published between 1848 (the date of the first women's rights convention) and 1970, the bibliography includes books, articles, dissertations, pamphlets, and government publications. Relevant manuscript collections and movement periodicals both are listed with indexes. The volume is partially annotated.

347 Rowbotham, Sheila. *Women's Liberation and Revolution.* London: Falling Wall Press, 1973. 24pp. This bibliography was compiled as part of the research for Rowbotham's book *Women: Resistance and Revolution.* It includes books, pamphlets, and articles which explore the relationship between feminism and revolutionary politics. It is organized by subject and includes materials published up to February 1972.

348 U.S. Library of Congress. *List of Recent Books on Feminism.* Washington, 1915. Out of print.

349 ———. *List of References on the General Federation of Women's Clubs.* Washington, 1916. Out of print.

350 ———. *List of References on Woman Suffrage.* Washington, 1913. Out of print.

351 ———. *List of References on Woman's Movement in England.* Washington, 1922. Out of print.

352 Winslow, Barbara. *Women's Liberation: Black Women, Working Women, Revolutionary Feminism.* Highland Park: Sun Press, 1976. 32pp. This brief bibliography has its limitations. Sun Press, the publisher, is the publications division of International Socialists and so the bibliography shows a small, but noticeable bias. A more annoying problem is the occasional incomplete citation. Other miscellaneous typing errors, incorrect dates, and so on, leave one questioning the bibliography's reliability.

Work

The participation of women in the labor force and the discrimination against them as workers have been key issues in the women's movement —and the subject of many a volume as evidenced by the size of this section. With thirty-nine entries, it is second only to the general section. There are bibliographies here on a number of specific topics concerning the woman at work: part-time employment, equal pay for equal work, working mothers, night work, nontraditional occupations, the minimum wage. Several bibliographies cover the literature on legal matters relating to employment: equal employment opportunity, discrimination, affirmative action. Also included in this section are bibliographies on women who work but are not paid—homemakers and volunteers.

SEE ALSO: Economics; Professions.

353 Almquist, Elizabeth M. "Review Essay: Women in the Labor Force." *Signs* 2(4):843–855, Summer 1977.

354 Bayefsky, Evelyn. "Women and the Status of Part-Time Work: A Review and Annotated Bibliography." *Ontario Library Review* 58:124–141, June 1974.

355 ———. "Women and Work: A Selection of Books and Articles." *Ontario Library Review* 56:79–90, June 1972. This annotated list, which is quite selective, covers books, pamphlets, and periodicals. It is good for references on Canadian women, though some American publications are listed.

356 Bickner, Mei Liang. *Women at Work: An Annotated Bibliography*. Los Angeles: University of California, Manpower Research Center, Institute of Industrial Relations, 1974. n.p. This bibliography is selective, including material of major importance published on working women in the United States through 1973. It is designed with researchers and serious students in mind. Subheads are: General, Historical Development, Education and Training, Working Women, Occupations, Special Groups, Public Policy, and Bibliographies. There are four indexes: author, subject, title, and KWIC (Key-Word-In-Context).

110

357   Catalyst. *InSight Bibliography Series.* Catalyst, a research and publishing organization concerned with women's employment, has produced a series of brief (the longest is six pages) bibliographies on a wide range of issues surrounding the working woman. Currently, there are approximately forty bibliographies available, with titles such as *Absenteeism and Turnover of Women Workers, Child-Care Deductions, Alternative Work Patterns,* and *Women in Academia* (or one of several other careers). Most of the current set was compiled in 1975, but an update is in progress as of this writing. This series is an excellent source of information on new trends and issues in the employment of women. Write for a publications/price list.

358   Center for Women Policy Studies. *Resource Listing: Wage-Earning Women.* Washington, n.d. 8pp. Out of print. This brief listing is in five sections: General, Blue Collar Workers, Statistics, Unions, and Vocational Education.

359   Elkin, Anna. *The Emerging Role of Mature Women: Basic Background Data in Employment and Continuing Education.* New York: Federation Employment and Guidance Service, 1976. 20pp. Elkin's bibliography includes ''relevant, free and inexpensive'' materials on the mature woman, women's education, and women's employment for the period 1969–1975. It is a straight alphabetical listing with no subject index, which makes it a bit difficult to use. Nevertheless, the annotations are helpful and a wide variety of material is covered.

360   Felmley, Jenrose. *Working Women: Homemakers and Volunteers: An Annotated Selected Bibliography.* Washington: Business and Professional Women's Foundation, 1975. 25pp. The introduction to this bibliography is a review essay on the literature. There are eighty-two entries listed alphabetically by main entry.

361   Feminist Theory Collective. *American Women: Our Lives and Labor, An Annotated Bibliography of Women and Work in the U.S., 1900–1975.* Eugene: Amazon Reality, 1976. 36pp. This bibliography comes, as many do, from a feminist study group

anxious to share the results of its work. The majority of works listed are on women and work in the twentieth century, but there are two short sections on general historical works and the nineteenth century. The bibliography is selective; criteria for inclusion were readability, availability, inclusion of minority women. Material on housework as work was sought, as were personal accounts and fiction. There is a general emphasis throughout on women in social movements and union organizing. The annotations are quite good.

362 Foreman, Jo Ann T. *Women: A Selected Annotated Bibliography on Their Equal Opportunity and Employment.* Baton Rouge: Louisiana State University, College of Business Administration, Division of Research, 1973. 20 pp. Foreman has divided her bibliography into two parts: an annotated listing of twenty citations to books and articles and a listing of approximately 175 additional citations (the first twenty repeat) which are not annotated. The second section is divided into subcategories by form: books, articles, government documents, and miscellaneous (mostly unpublished) papers. There is no introduction, so we have no explanation of how or why the twenty citations were chosen for annotation. Most of the materials listed are fairly recent—concentrating in the 1960s and 70s—though the books section includes some works published in the early part of the century and the 1890s. The subject coverage is broad, including overviews of women's labor force participation and status, analysis of and remedies for employment discrimination, and women in business and management.

363 Glaser-Malbin, Nona. "Review Essay: Housework." *Signs* 1(4): 905–922, Summer 1976.

364 Haist, Dianne. *Equal Pay for Work of Equal Value: A Selected Bibliography.* Toronto: Ontario Ministry of Labor, Research Branch, 1976. 15pp.

365 Hallowell, Ila M. *Employment Discrimination Against Women, A Selected Annotated Bibliography.* Albany: New York State Library, Legislative Reference Library, 1972. 41pp.

366 Kievit, Mary Bach. *Review and Synthesis of Research on Women in the World of Work*. Columbus: ERIC Clearinghouse on Vocational and Technical Education, 1972. (ED 066 553).

367 Matthews, Catherine J. and Marnie Shea. *Affirmative Action; A Selected Bibliography*. Toronto: Ontario Ministry of Labour, Research Library, 1975. 17pp.

368 McKim, Joanne. *Women and Employment Bibliography*. Santa Ana, 1973. 33pp. Out of print. McKim describes her bibliography as an "extensive, though not yet complete list of sources" on women at work in America from Colonial times to the present (1973). It is divided into sections by chronology, and there is considerable variation among them. For instance, the first and largest chronological category, Colonial Period to 1890, has only twenty-nine citations, while the smallest of the other sections, 1915 to 1930, has sixty-nine citations for the fifteen year period. *Women and Employment* is perhaps better described as an extensive list of sources on women and work in the twentieth century (nearly 475 entries out of the total 550).

369 Moore, Louise. *Occupations for Girls and Women: Selected References, July 1943-June 1948*. Washington: U.S. Department of Labor, Women's Bureau, 1942. Out of print.

370 Moser, Collette and Deborah Johnson. *Rural Women Workers in the Twentieth Century: An Annotated Bibliography*. East Lansing: Michigan State University, College of Agriculture and Natural Resources, Department of Agricultural Economics, 1973. 63pp. This bibliography includes all formats of material (books, articles, etc.), with some pieces dating back to the nineteenth century. The authors have defined "rural" to include both farm and nonfarm work, household and manual labor. Different sections cover women's preparation for work, the qualitative and quantitative aspects of their labor force participation, their problems in working, farm and women's organizations, and international trends.

371 Nicolas, Suzanne. *Bibliography on Women Workers 1861-1965*. Geneva: International Labour Office, Central Library and

Documentation Branch, 1970. 252pp. Most of the nearly 1,800 works cited in this bibliography are either government documents or publications of the International Labour Office itself. The volume is divided into eleven broad subject sections. It includes many foreign language works. There are subject, geographical, and author indexes that were computer-generated.

372 Pinto, Patrick R. and Jeanne O. Buchmeier. *Problems and Issues in the Employment of Minority, Disadvantaged and Female Groups: An Annotated Bibliography.* ERIC, 1973. 62pp. (ED 083 339). This bibliography lists selected materials published from July 2, 1965—the effective date of Title VII of the 1964 Civil Rights Act—to 1972. It includes books, articles, reports, and government documents.

373 Samuels, Victoria. *Nowhere to Be Found, A Literature Review and Annotated Bibliography on White Working Class Women.* New York: Institute on Pluralism and Group Identity, 1975. 29 pp. While it is only a beginning, Samuels's literature review is both interesting and helpful. She points to the paucity of material on the working-class woman and offers some explanations. Her underlying theme is the lack of communication and understanding between the women's movement and working-class women. She blames the stereotyped media image of each—and both groups' willingness to believe in it. She discusses only eight works in the literature review and annotates in depth an additional twenty-nine in the bibliography section. Nevertheless, this is a valuable compilation.

374 Schroeder, Paul E. *Women in the World of Work: A Bibliography of ERIC Documents.* ERIC, 1973. 29pp. (ED 083 479).

375 Soltow, Martha J. and Mary K. Wery. *American Women and the Labor Movement, 1825-1974.* Metuchen: Scarecrow Press, 1976. 247pp. This revised edition of Soltow's bibliography brings the inclusive dates up to 1974—the original edition covered the period up to 1935. It is selective, annotated, and includes books, articles, pamphlets, and U.S. government documents. The section on women in unions has been expanded, a section on the Coalition of Labor Union Women added. Materials on employ-

ment discrimination and protective legislation receive less emphasis as they are covered in other bibliographies. An appendix lists archival sources on women and labor. There is a cross-reference, a subject, and an author index. (Original edition: Soltow, Martha J. "Women in Labor Unions in the United States, 1825–1935; A Bibliography." *Review of Radical Political Economics* 4:150–154, July 1972.)

376 Spiegel, Jeanne. *Working Mothers: A Selected Annotated Bibliography*. Washington: Business and Professional Women's Foundation, 1968. 24pp. The materials covered are those about and of interest to working mothers published within the last ten to fifteen years. Books, pamphlets, reports, periodical articles, microfilm, and tape recordings are included. The citations are arranged into chapters by type of material and then listed alphabetically by author. Everything listed is available in the Foundation library. Annotations are descriptive.

377 U.S. Department of Health, Education and Welfare, Office of Education, Bureau of Occupational and Adult Education. *Women in Non-Traditional Occupations—A Bibliography*. Washington, 1976. 189pp. Because there is no detailed, widely-accepted definition of which occupations are traditional or non-traditional for women, a working definition was developed for the preparation of this bibliography. The percentage of women in the labor force in 1970—the cut-off publication date for inclusion of materials—was established from government statistics. This figure, thirty-eight percent, was then used as a base, so that any field less than thirty-eight percent female was regarded as nontraditional. The materials collected using these guidelines were organized into three categories: Overview, Women in the Skilled Trades, and Women in Professional Occupations. The third section is by far the largest. The annotations are descriptive only. There are author, title, and subject indexes.

378 U.S. Department of Labor, Bureau of Labor Statistics. *Where to Find BLS Statistics on Women*. Washington, 1978. This slim pamphlet is an excellent guide that takes one by the hand through the maze of government publications on working women. There are statistical areas covered in four sections: Labor

Force Status, Employment and Unemployment; Earnings and Hours of Work; Education; Membership in Labor Organizations. The information is organized into four columns for easy access: Characteristics of Data Desired, Where Published, Frequency of Publication, and Most Recent Issue. Complete ordering information is given in a section at the back. For anyone who needs access to government statistics, this is a lifesaver.

379 U.S. Department of Labor, Women's Bureau. *Bibliography on Night Work for Women.* Washington, 1946. 39pp. Out of print. The bibliography covers reports from government agencies, research agencies, academic institutions, personnel officers, and psychologists, primarily from the years 1936 to 1946. The selections are annotated, and the annotations are quite long, including tables. The citations are arranged by country—United States, Great Britain, and Australia—and subdivided into government and private sources under each. There is a final section on international publications.

380 ———. *Employment of Older Women: An Annotated Bibliography.* Washington, 1954. 89pp. Out of print. Included in this bibliography are articles, books, and conference papers dealing with hiring practices, psychological barriers, and work performance in the employment of older women. The annotations, which are quite long and detailed, are listed alphabetically by author and are numbered; access is through the subject index.

381 ———. *Employment of Older Women: An Annotated Bibliography: Hiring Practices, Attitudes, Work Performance.* Washington, 1957. 83pp. Out of print.

382 ———. *Guide to Sources of Data on Women and Women Workers for the U.S. and Regions, States and Local Areas.* Washington, 1972. 15pp. Compiled to help those drafting affirmative action plans find statistics to back up their cases, this bibliography indicates whether or not each publication includes data based on sex, race, educational attainment, labor force participation, occupation, and industry. Publications are listed by the following subjects: population, education, civic labor force and unemployment, occupation and industry, and labor force

reserve. Also indicated is whether or not data relates to United States, region, state, or Standard Metropolitan Statistical Area (metropolitan areas of more than fifty thousand population).

383 ———. *List of References on Minimum Wage for Women in the U.S. and Canada.* Washington, 1925. 42pp. Out of print. This bibliography is international in scope and includes articles, government reports, court decisions, and industry and union bulletins. There are occasional annotations. The bibliography has been divided into chapters which include: Bibliographies; U.S., General; U.S., States Which Have Adopted Minimum Wage Laws; U.S., Other States; Canada.

384 U.S. Library of Congress. *Brief List on Legislation and Court Decisions Protecting Women Workers.* Washington, 1916. Out of print.

385 ———. *List of References on Women's Work and Wages.* Washington, 1909. Out of print.

386 ———. *Select List of References on a Minimum Wage for Women.* Washington, 1913. Out of print.

387 ———. *Select List of References on the Work of Women in Civil Reform.* Washington, 1913. Out of print.

388 ———. *Select List of References Relating to Night Work for Women.* Washington, 1913. Out of print.

389 ———. *Select List of Works on Women in Business.* Washington, 1909. Out of print.

390 ———. *A Short List of References on the Wages of Women in the United States.* Washington, 1923. Out of print.

391 Ward, Dennis F. *Sex Discrimination in Employment, 1969–1975: A Selective Bibliography.* Part I. Sacramento: California State Law Library, 1976. 15pp. Ward's compilation updates a 1969 version of this bibliography prepared by Marija Hughes. Part I covers notes (brief factual summaries) and comments

(analysis, interpretation—a longer treatment) published in scholarly journals on the U.S. statutory and case law involving sex discrimination in employment. Only cases involving federal law have been included, and only those articles published between 1969 and 1975. The bibliography is arranged by case, rather than title or author, with all citations to relevant articles listed under each. The major points and arguments of each case are given, which makes the bibliography very useful to the uninitiated legal researcher. Part II was never published.

Author Index

The number following the author's name refers to the publication's entry in this bibliography.

Title Index

The number following the title refers to the publication's entry in this bibliography.

Publishers

ABC-Clio
  Riviera Campus
  2040 A.P.S., Box 4397
  Santa Barbara, CA 93103
Alabama, University of
  Center for Correctional Psychology
  P. O. Box 2968
  University, AL 35468
Amazon Reality
  P. O. Box 95
  Eugene, OR 97401
American Alliance for Health,
    Physical Education and Recreation
  1201 16th St. N.W.
  Washington, DC 20036
American Council of Voluntary
    Agencies for Foreign Services
  Technical Assistance Information
    Clearinghouse
  200 Park Ave. South
  New York, NY 10003
American Library Association
  c/o Barbara Gittings
  P. O. Box 2383
  Philadelphia, PA 19103
American Pyschological Association
  Journal Supplement Abstract Service
  1200 17th St. N.W.
  Washington, DC 20036
Anshen Publishing
  See: Cowan, Belita
Arno Press
  3 Park Ave.
  New York, NY 10016
Association of American Colleges
  Project on the Status and Education
    of Women
  1818 R St. N.W.
  Washington, DC 20009
Auburn Theological Seminary
  3041 Broadway
  New York, NY 10027

Bart, Pauline
  Department of Psychiatry
  Illinois Medical Center
  P. O. Box 6998
  Chicago, IL 60680
Behavioral Publications
  72 Fifth Ave.
  New York, NY 10011
Biblio Press
  P. O. Box 22
  Fresh Meadows, NY 11365
Bloch Publishing
  915 Broadway
  New York, NY 10010
Bowker, R. R.
  1180 Ave. of the Americas
  New York, NY 10036
Bowling Green State University
    Libraries
  Bowling Green, OH 43402
Business and Professional Women's
    Foundation
  2012 Massachusetts Ave. N.W.
  Washington, DC 20036

California State College Library
  Dominguez Hills, CA 90747
California State Law Library
  Library-Courts Bldg.
  Sacramento, CA 95809
California State University
  J.F.K. Memorial Library
  Los Angeles, CA 90024
California State University
  Library
  Sacramento, CA 95819
California, University of
  Chicano Studies Center
  Los Angeles, CA 90024
California, University of
  Chicano Studies Library

3408 Dwinelle Hall
Berkeley, CA 94720
California, University of
Library Administration
P. O. Box 19557
Irvine, CA 92713
California, University of
Manpower Research Center
Institute of Industrial Relations
Los Angeles, CA 90024
Canadian Newsletter of Research on
Women
Department of Sociology
Ontario Institute for Studies in
Education
252 Bloor Street West
Toronto, Ontario M5S 1V6
Canada
Catalyst
14 East 60th Street
New York, NY 10022
Center for the American Woman and
Politics
Rutgers University
New Brunswick, NJ 08901
Center for Women's Studies and
Services
908 F Street
San Diego, CA 92101
Cisler, Lucinda
P. O. Box 240
Planetarium Station
New York, NY 10024
College Entrance Examination Board
Publications Order Office
P. O. Box 592
Princeton, NJ 08540
Common Women Collective, The
5 Upland Road
Cambridge, MA 02140
Connecticut, University of
Library Acquisitions Department
Box U–T
Storrs, CT 06268
Council of Planning Librarians
P. O. Box 229
Monticello, IL 61856

Cowan, Belita
3821 T St. N.W.
Washington, DC 20007
Current Bibliography Series
P. O. Box 2709
San Diego, CA 92112

Education Commission of the States
1860 Lincoln St.
Denver, CO 80203
Entropy Ltd.
215 Tennyson Ave.
Pittsburgh, PA 15213
Episcopal Diocese of Pennsylvania
1700 Market St.
Philadelphia, PA 19103
ERIC
Document Reproduction Service
P. O. Box 190
Arlington, CA 22210

Falling Wall Press
See: The Feminist Press
Farians, Elizabeth
6125 Webbland Pl.
Cincinnati, OH 45213
Federation Employment and Guidance
Service
215 Park Ave. South
New York, NY 10003
Feminist Press, The
P. O. Box 334
Old Westbury, NY 11568

Garland
545 Madison Ave.
New York, NY 10022
General Learning Press
Silver Burdett
250 James St.
Morristown, NJ 07960
Glide Publications
330 Ellis St.
San Francisco, CA 94102
Graduate Theological Union
Office of Women's Affairs

2465 Le Conte Ave.
Berkeley, CA 94709
Greenwood Press
51 Riverside Ave.
Westport, CT 06880

Hall, G. K.
70 Lincoln St.
Boston, MA 02111
Harvard University
Department of Philosophy
Cambridge, MA 02138
ATTN: Louise Anthony
Hawaii, University of
See: Sturgeon, Susan
Health Sciences Publications
451 Greenwich St.
New York, NY 10013
Henriques, Cynthia
See: Bart, Pauline
Hera Press
P. O. Box 18037
Cleveland, OH 44118
Hughes Press
500 23rd St. N.W.
Washington, DC 20037

Institute for Scientific Analysis
See: Northwestern University
Institute on Pluralism and Group
Identity
165 E. 56th St.
New York, NY 10022
International Labor Office
1750 New York Ave.
Washington, DC 20006
International Reading Association
400 Barksdale
Newark, DE 19711
Iowa State University Library
Ames, IA 50010
ATTN: Photoduplication

Kent State University
School of Library Science
Kent, OH 44240

King, Judith D.
3327 Campus View Apartments
Allendale, MI 49401
Knopf, Alfred A.
201 East 50th St.
New York, NY 10022
KNOW, Inc.
P. O. Box 86031
Pittsburgh, PA 15221

Ladder, The
See: Naiad Press
Lake Forest College
Donnelly Library
Lake Forest, IL 60045
Louisiana State University
College of Business Administration
Division of Research
Baton Rouge, LA 70803

McMaster University Library Press
Mills Memorial Library
McMaster University
Hamilton, Ont. L8S 4L6
Canada
McMaster University Medical Centre
Hamilton, Ont. L8S 4L6
Canada
Maferr Foundation
140 W. 57th St.
New York, NY 10019
Massachusetts Institute of Technology
Human Studies Collection
Humanities Library
Cambridge, MA 02139
Michigan State University
College of Agricultural and Natural
Resources
Department of Agricultural
Economics
East Lansing, MI 48823
Michigan State University Libraries
East Lansing, MI 48823
Michigan, University of
Center for Population Planning
Ann Arbor, MI 48104

Michigan, University of
  Institute for Social Research
  Center for Political Studies
  Ann Arbor, MI 48105
Moulton, Janice
  See: Harvard University

Naiad Press
  20 Rue Jacob Acres
  Bates City, MO 64011
National Association for Women Deans,
    Administrators and Counselors
  1028 Connecticut Ave N.W.
  Washington, DC 20036
National Center For Education Statistics
  400 Maryland Ave. S.W.
  Washington, DC 20202
National Institute on Drug Abuse
  Clearinghouse for Drug Information
  1400 Rockville Pike
  Rockville, MD 20852
National Organization for Women,
    Task Force on Older Women
  See: Glide Publications
National Technical Information Service
  5285 Port Royal Rd.
  Springfield, VA 22151
Neal-Schuman Publishing
  64 University Pl.
  New York, NY 10003
New Horizons Press
  P. O. Box 1758
  Chico, CA 95926
New TransCentury Foundation
  Secretariat for Women in
    Development
  1789 Columbia Rd. N.W.
  Washington, DC 20009
New York State Library
  Legislative Reference Library
    Albany, NY 12223
Northern Illinois University Library
  Education Cluster
  De Kalb, IL 60115
  ATTN: Pat McMillan

Northwestern University
  The Program on Women
  619 Emerson St.
  Evanston, IL 60201
Northwestern University Library
  Evanston, IL 60201
Nower, Joyce
  See: Center for Women's Studies and
    Services

Ohio State University
  Center for Human Resource Research
  1375 Perry St.
  Columbus, OH 43201
Ohio State University
  Center for Vocational and Technical
    Education
  980 Kinnear
  Columbus, OH 43212
Ontario Ministry of Labour
  Research Library
  400 University Ave.
  Toronto, Ont.
  Canada
Overseas Development Council
  1717 Massachusetts Ave. N.W.
  Washington, DC 20036

Pennsylvania State University
  Agricultural Experiment Station
  Department of Agricultural
    Economics and Rural Sociology
  University Park, PA 16802
Pool, Jeannie G.
  P. O. Box 436
  Ansonia Sta.
  New York, NY 10027

Reference Service Press
  9023 Alcott St.
  Los Angeles, CA 90035
Research Group One
  2743 Maryland Ave.
  Baltimore, MD 21218

Research Publications
  12 Lunar Dr.
  Woodbridge, CT 06525
Rochester, University of
  Management Library
  Rochester, NY 14627

Sage Publications
  275 S. Beverly Dr.
  Beverly Hills, CA 90212
St. Louis Feminist Research Project
  4431 McPherson
  St. Louis, MO 63108
San Jose State University Library
  Collection Coordinator
  250 S. 4th St.
  San Jose, CA 95192
Sarah Lawrence College
  Library
  Bronxville, NY 10708
Sarah Lawrence College
  Women's Studies Program
  Bronxville, NY 10708
Saskatchewan, University of
  Saskatoon, Sas.
  Canada
Scarecrow Press
  52 Liberty St.
  Metuchen, NJ 08840
Signs
  University of Chicago Press
  5801 Ellis Ave.
  Chicago, IL 60637
Sturgeon, Susan
  45 Blaisdell Dr.
  Carlisle, MA 07141
Sun Press
  See: Hera Press
Superintendent of Documents
  Government Printing Office
  Washington, DC 20402

Texas, University of
  Center for Middle Eastern Studies
  Austin, TX 78712

Texas, University of
  School of Social Work
  Center for Social Work Research
  Austin, TX 78712
Thomas, Charles C.
  301 Lawrence
  Springfield, IL 62703
Toronto, University of
  John P. Robarts Research Library
  Toronto, Ont. M5S 1A5
  Canada

Unipub
  P. O. Box 433
  Murray Hill Sta.
  New York, NY 10016
United Methodist Church
  Board of Church and Society
  Department of Drug and Alcohol
    Concerns
  100 Maryland Ave. N.E.
  Washington, DC 20002
United Nations
  See: Unipub
U. S. Air Force Academy Library
  See: National Technical Information
    Service
U. S. Department of Health, Education
    and Welfare
  Office of Education
  Bureau of Occupational and Adult
    Education
  Washington, DC 20202
  ATTN: Deborah Ashford
U. S. Department of Labor
  Bureau of Labor Statistics
  Washington, DC 20212
U. S. Department of Labor
  Women's Bureau
  Office of the Secretary
  Washington, DC 20210
U. S. Department of Labor Library
  See: Superintendent of Documents
U. S. Library of Congress
  Congressional Research Service
  Governments Division
  Washington, DC 20540

Washington State Library
  Institutional Library Services
  Documents Division
  Olympia, WA 98504
Whitson Publishing
  P. O. Box 322
  Troy, NY 12181
Wisconsin, University of
  School of Social Welfare
  Midwest Parent-Child Welfare
    Resource Center
  P. O. Box 413
  Milwaukee, WI 53201
Wittenburg University
  Information Services
  Springfield, OH 45504
Womanbooks
  201 W. 92nd St.
  New York, NY 10025
Womanpress
  P. O. Box 59330
  Chicago, IL 60645

Womanspace: Feminist Therapy
  Collective
  636 Beacon St.
  Boston, MA 02215
Women and Literature Collective
  P. O. Box 441
  Cambridge, MA 02138
Women's Educational Equity
    Communications Network
  Far West Laboratory
  1855 Folsom St.
  San Francisco, CA 94103
Women's Studies Abstracts
  Rush Publishing
  P. O. Box 1
  Rush, NY 14543

Zenger Publishing
  P. O. Box 31061
  Washington, DC 20031

About the Author

Jane Williamson, co-author of *Feminist Resources for Schools and Colleges: A Guide to Curricular Materials* and *Women's Action Almanac: A Complete Resource Guide,* received her M.S. degree from the School of Library Service, Columbia University. Former Managing Editor of the *Women's Studies Newsletter,* at present she is the Director of Information Services at the Women's Action Alliance, a national center for information on women's issues and programs.

About The Feminist Press

The Feminist Press offers alternatives in education and in literature. Founded in 1970, this nonprofit, tax-exempt educational and publishing organization works to eliminate sexual stereotypes in books and schools, providing instead a new or neglected literature with a broader vision of human potential. Our books include reprints of important works about women, feminist biographies of women, and nonsexist children's books. Curricular materials, bibliographies, directories, and a newsletter provide information and support for women's studies at every educational level. Our inservice projects help teachers develop new methods to encourage students to become their best and freest selves. Through our publications and projects we can begin to recreate the forgotten history of women and begin to create a more humane and equitable society for the future.

This book was made possible by the work of many people, including The Feminist Press Staff and Board. The Board, the decision-making body of the Press, includes all staff members and other individuals who have an ongoing relationship to The Feminist Press: Phyllis Arlow, Jeanne Bracken, Brenda Carter, Toni Cerutti, Ranice Crosby, Sue Davidson, Michelina Fitzmaurice, Jeanne Ford, Shirley Frank, Merle Froschl, Barbara Gore, Brett Harvey, Ilene Hertz, Florence Howe, Paul Lauter, Carol Levin, Corrine Lucido, Mary Mulrooney, Ethel J. Phelps, Elizabeth Phillips, Karen Raphael, Helen Schrader, Merryl Sloane, Susan Trowbridge, Sandy Weinbaum, Sharon Wigutoff, Jane Williamson, Sophie Zimmerman.

Other Books from The Feminist Press's Clearinghouse on Women's Studies

GENERAL EDUCATION

Feminist Resources for Schools and Colleges

Merle Froschl and Jane Williamson, eds. (Revised ed. 1977). A selective guide to curricular materials at every level from the elementary school to the university—for teachers, students, librarians, and parents who want to challenge sexism in education and create nonsexist and feminist curriculum.

Women's Studies Newsletter

A quarterly published by The Feminist Press and the National Women's Studies Association. Contains articles on women's studies at all levels of education: new programs, innovative courses, teaching techniques, curricular materials, book reviews, conference reports, bibliography, job information.

ELEMENTARY EDUCATION

Books for Today's Children

Jeanne Bracken and Sharon Wigutoff, eds. (1979). Critically annotated list of two hundred recent picture books. Subject index includes Working Mothers, Handicaps, Contemporary Grandparents, Multi-Racial, Adoption, Single Parents, Sensitive Males, Adventurous Females.

Nonsexist Curricular Materials for Elementary Schools

Laurie Olsen Johnson, ed. (1974). A collection of materials for the elementary teacher and student, including quizzes, checklists, bibliographies, workbook, model units.

SECONDARY EDUCATION

Changing Learning, Changing Lives

Barbara Gates, Susan Klaw, and Adria Steinberg. (1979). A comprehensive women's studies curriculum developed by The Group School, an alternative high school for working-class youth in Cambridge, Massachusetts. Includes nine thematic units plus suggestions for role plays, trips, interviewing, making a film, and publishing a newspaper.

High School Feminist Studies
Carol Ahlum and Jacqueline Fralley, compilers. Florence Howe, ed. (1976). A collection of curricular materials in women's studies for and from high schools including essays, bibliographies, teaching units.

Strong Women
Deborah Silverton Rosenfelt, ed. (1976). Annotated bibliography of widely available paperbacks to help the teacher supplement the male-biased curriculum: anthologies, autobiography, novels, short stories, drama, poetry.

HIGHER EDUCATION

Who's Who and Where in Women's Studies
Tamar Berkowitz, Jean Mangi, and Jane Williamson, eds. (1974). Complete directory of women's studies programs, courses, and teachers, arranged by institution, department, and instructor.

Female Studies VI
Closer to the Ground: Women's Classes, Criticism, Programs—1972
Nancy Hoffman, Cynthia Secor, and Adrian Tinsley, eds., for the Commission on the Status of Women of the Modern Language Association. (1972). Essays on women's studies in the classroom, literary criticism from a feminist perspective, course materials.

Female Studies VII
Going Strong: New Courses/New Programs
Deborah Rosenfelt, ed. (1973). Syllabi for over sixty recent women's studies courses; descriptions of twelve new programs. Introductory essay assessing recent developments in women's studies.

Female Studies IX
Teaching about Women in the Foreign Languages
Sidoni Cassirer, ed., for the Commission on the Status of Women of the Modern Language Association. (1975). Listings and outlines of courses with a focus on women offered by departments of French, Spanish, and German in colleges and universities across the country.

Female Studies X
Student Work—Learning to Speak
Deborah Silverton Rosenfelt, ed. (1975). The fruits of some five years of undergraduate women's studies courses on campuses across the country: a first play, a ''group autobiography,'' poems, short stories, papers.

DATE DUE

APR 2 1982			
MAR 8 1983			
DEC 1 7 1985			
OCT 28 '86			
MAR 1 5 1988			

DEMCO 38-297